Also by Andrew McGregor

Simply Learn Tarot
The only book beginners need to
start reading the easy way

A Tarot of You
Finding yourself in the cards

Coming Winter 2016
Reading the Thoth Tarot
A practical guide to divining with
the Thoth Tarot

A Tarot of You!

Your life belongs in tarot!
Welcome to a journey through the
trumps as they apply to you
and your life.

By Andrew McGregor

Dedication

To my super editor and creative muse. Hanlon, for being so supportive of my work – and helping shape it both by asking great questions and by correcting mistakes.

Also, to Dy and Sherryl, for being super guinea pigs.

Copyright 2016 Andrew McGregor. No part may be reproduced without written permission. Please don't share this with anyone. It is available for purchase at my website thehermitslamp.com and other places.

Images used with permission

"Death" by Joanna Powell Colbert from the *Gaian Tarot*

The Moon by Dy Langdon

Tarot Waiting to Happen images by Andrew McGregor

"The Reader" by Andrew McGregor (Cover Image)

Images used under license

Tarot card images in this book are from the *CBD Tarot de Marseille* created by Yoav Ben-Dov, www.cbdtarot.com. Used with permission.

CONTENTS

Foreword	1
Introduction	3
The Fool	12
The Magician	20
The High Priestess	30
The Empress	38
The Emperor	48
The Hierophant	58
The Lovers	66
The Chariot	74
Justice	84
The Hermit	92
The Wheel of Fortune	100
Strength	108
The Hanged Man	116
Death	126
Temperance	134
The Devil	142
The Tower	150
The Star	160
The Moon	170
The Sun	180
Judgement	188
The World	198
Appendix	207
Credits	209

Foreword

by Barbara Moore

Whenever I meet fellow tarot lovers who believe that each card has one basic meaning and that there is only one valid way to depict that meaning, it makes me really sad. Those people are denying themselves the joy of discovery and the thrill of exploration. Instead of thinking of the cards as static (which historically, they haven't been, so why would they be now?), imagine that they are portals opening into vast worlds of meaning, wisdom, and potential. Each card includes multitudes of possibility. To think that only one set of symbols and one composition can effectively represent this vastness is, well, kind of silly.

Also, there is the whole issue of symbolism. Historic decks use symbols that worked for their culture, which was usually defined by location and time. Symbols are not immutable. They do not stay the same from the beginning of human existence until the end. Heck, just looking at the history of the swastika symbol will show you how much a symbol's meaning can change. The superstar of the tarot world, the Rider-Waite-Smith deck, is based on Victorian-era Gnostic-Christian symbols that do not necessarily reflect contemporary experiences. Most of us did not know, for example, what a Hierophant was when we picked up our first deck. How can something be an effective symbol if the viewer doesn't even know what it is, let alone what it means? Symbols work because they mean something, immediately, to the viewer.

In addition to the problem of changing symbols in general, there is another issue that is unique to us in contemporary Western Civilization: we do not have a very well-developed and commonly accepted, shared symbol system. This creates a lot of problems for our culture, but in terms of tarot, it means that designing a deck that will be symbolically relevant to a large group of people is really challenging. People often ask me about the future of tarot, and I've never had a really good answer – until now.

Andrew's book *A Tarot of You* may very well be the future of tarot. If we cannot find a shared symbol set, then let's each make our own. Reading Andrew's book really was a "duh!" moment for me. My own beliefs about tarot include: everything about your tarot practice should reflect your own belief system. Andrew takes this further: your tarot deck should reflect your own belief system. And he takes that idea even further: not only should it reflect your own beliefs, but it should also reflect your own experiences. These experiences are gained through Andrew's masterful guidance. For each card, he creates an environment that you explore for six days, culminating with a completed card on the sacred seventh day. At the end of the process, you have a Major Arcana deck that not only reflects your beliefs but also incorporates new wisdom gained through direct experience.

Let me tell you my favourite part of this process. Part of the process includes being willing to gamble. Use dice. Court chance. Invite randomness. Evoke the transformative energy of the Trickster. Adding a little Trickster to the mix is like adding a dollop of magic. And it keeps us honest. Instead of just making card images based on preconceived ideas, comfortable ideas, safe ideas, this smidgen of chaos forces us to look something new or unexpected square in the eyes and respond to it. That's spiritual growth gold right there.

Be brave and embrace the Trickster. Be creative and express the beauty of your spirit. Be smart and make your deck!

~ Barbara Moore

Introduction

First, I am very glad that you have bought this book. Wonderful. I have no doubt that magick will ensue. Secondly, we need to talk about how this works. I have some advice, suggestions, and guidelines to help you get the most out of doing this work.

The biggest piece of advice is that you can't make a wrong card! Whatever emerges will be exactly what it needs to be!

A few other guidelines are:

- **Trust the process** – Every bit of this process has been designed to get you to a great deck that will speak to you for your whole life. It won't always make sense as you are doing it, but in time it will reveal its mysteries to you.

- **Think about the end result before you start making art** – Do you want a printed deck you can work with? Awesome. There are so many easy ways to go about it. You could print it at home on card stock. Printing at home is easy to figure out. Just try it and make adjustments. Local copy shops can print it really affordably, as can a variety of online services geared towards playing card and tarot deck custom printing. Each of these will have their own approach and requirements. If you are using an outside service find out what they would like from you to make sure you don't have to recreate anything later on. Don't worry, though. It is easy. The "file set up" in the appendix section will walk you through the process.

- **Avoid excuses and problems** – Most blocks around this work are easy to see coming. Make sure you set aside time to work. Make sure you have the supplies you need. At some point, your resistance will try to use every obstacle as a reason to **not** do the work. Preparation is the cure for this.

- **Don't fall behind** – It is easy to let life, or our resistance to the process, derail something like this. It might help to get an accountability buddy. It is easy to get behind and then just stop all together. At the time of publication, there is a Facebook group for people working on this. Email me to join. *Nothing online is eternal so this might not be there forever.*

- **Don't repeat days** – Each day is meant to be done once. Don't go back and redo them. There are no wrong answers. Perfection is boring. What needs to surface will come up later. Trust the process.

- **What about my great ideas?** This kind of work sparks a flow of creativity. Which is awesome. Decide now where those ideas can go for later review. A notebook, a file on your computer, whatever. Just don't get pulled off track by them.

Are You Ready to Make Magick?

This process relies on magick. *Seriously.* Tarot at its best is inspired by spirit and augmented by our creativity and knowledge. How it truly works is a mysterious process that is beyond defining. By using magick, or, if you prefer, non-rational methods, to both make decisions and gather information, you will be able to reveal deeper truths, access clearer archetypes, and bypass your expectations in the creation process to produce cards that speak to you for the rest of your life.

When working magically it is important to follow a few guidelines and set a few limits too.

Have a clear request.

If the process calls for you to ask a question of the cards or your spirit, make that question specific. Keep it short and simple – if you can't easily remember it, it is not yet simple enough.

"Spirit, I need you to reveal the meaning of the dog on The Fool card in the next 24 hours" is great. "Hey, uh spirit, I was looking at a card, and I don't know what it means. Does the dog say I will find love or work or what is going with that?" is obviously muddy.

Have a clear time frame in mind.

Looking for signs and synchronicities can be a bit unhinging if not contained. When every interaction could be a message from God, it becomes impossible to be sure which is the right one. Adding a time frame to your request helps avoid this problem. Especially where we are working on a schedule, ask for your answer within 24 hours.

Accept the answer even if you don't understand it.

Omens, prophecy, signs, dreams, and tarot are all complex communications that reveal their depth with time. I spend a lot of time in my reading practice helping people realize the gold in dreams they thought made no sense. Note your reaction to what comes up; it is a part of the message too, but don't allow your initial feelings to dismiss the symbol. Whatever comes up is perfect, whether or not you like it or understand it.

Synchronistic Whatchamacallit?

At the start of every card I am going to ask you to invoke a synchronicity in your life, using the tarot deck of your choosing to help you access what might be hiding in your subconscious. These instructions are included here in the Introduction because you will need to refer to them each week until the steps become internalized.

This might sound a bit "out there," but, with a bit of attention on your part, it should be pretty easy to do. Just follow these easy steps.

1. Grab your cards and your journal.

2. Take a few minutes to relax and centre yourself.

3. Say aloud: "I am here today to ask the universe to show me what I need to know about where my life and The Fool card (or card you are doing) intersect. I ask that you show me something in the world that will help me understand both this archetype and myself better. Please reveal to me – in the card I am about to draw – a clear sign that I can watch for, as I live my life over the next 24 hours, so I can recognize the moment you are speaking to me with certainty."

4. Draw a card face down so you don't see it.

5. Keeping relaxed, flip it over and note what stands out at first glance. Do not judge what you see, and definitely do not interpret the card. If it is a flower, write that down; if it a person, a colour, a shape, write that down.

6. Say, "Thank you universe. I will be watching for [say what you saw as the symbol] in the next 24 hours."

7. Watch for this cue in your life, and then take note of what is going on when you see it.

Tip #1 This process is really not about using the card meanings to read about this. We want a visual symbol to look for so we can be sure that what we are witnessing is a message from the universe. In this instance, it doesn't matter at all what the card means.

Tip #2 An example: I grabbed my Thoth deck and flipped the Empress. As I looked at the card, my eyes immediately went to the white bird. I thought of swans. So for the next 24 hours, I will be looking out for swans, and when I see one, I will note what is going on and interpret that situation as if it were a dream or a tarot card. It does not matter that I know this bird is actually a pelican. What matters is what I thought I saw on first glance.

Tip #3 What did I see? When you see your synchronistic cue in the world, pay attention. For example when I saw my swan, it was being fed by children at a park. The children were nervous, and the swan a bit reluctant. These are the ideas I need to look at in relationship to the card I am making. How does reluctance and nervousness relate to the card I am making? What symbol of those feelings might need to be on my card? Of course, I might also have seen the swan on a person's shirt, a sign, or any number of other places.

Rolling Dice?

I wanted to really include some magick through the power of chance in this process. It is too easy to simply create ideas we think are right that, in the end, are comfortable and limited in their power. So at some point in each card, you will be asked to roll a regular six-sided die to pick options for you. Please don't cheat yourself by rolling more than once per option. You are always welcome to not use the images or ideas you rolled for, but please make sure you consider them and include them in your process.

If you feel inclined, you may want to create a consecration ritual for your die. Put it on an altar. Light a candle beside it. Baptize it to your guardian angel. Here is a suggestion of what that might look like. Change any of it to make it more suited to your beliefs.

1. Gather a six-sided die, a bag or cloth to hold the die, an incense you like, your favourite tarot deck, some salt, and a candle.

2. Light your candle and incense.

3. Pull the four aces and put them in the four directions: wands in the south, cups in the west, disks in the north and swords in the east. Say, "I call on the wisdom of the four elements to bless this work."

4. Pull The Magician and put him on top of the deck in the centre of your table. "I call on my inner wisdom and guides to open clear channels of communication through all of this work."

5. Sprinkle the die with some salt. "I cleanse this instrument of chance that it may be made a clear vessel of spirit through the power of synchronicity."

6. Touch it to each of the aces, saying, "I invoke the power of wands so you may act correctly. I invoke the power of cups so you may bring emotional clarity. I invoke the power of disks so you may show me what is real. I invoke the power of swords so you may guide my thoughts to clarity."

7. Touch the die to The Magician and say, "I invoke the power of communication that brings mastery through wisdom. May all my efforts be blessed."

8. Hold the die in the incense and say, "May the power of aspiration hold fast."

9. Hold the die near the flame on the candle, saying, "May my light be revealed to me in its splendour."

10. Place the die in the cloth or bag and only bring it out when you are using it.

Building Your Images

This work is pretty fast paced. Unless you are free of the obligation of work, doing oil paintings like the masters, carving marble, or making large quilts are all unreasonable mediums to work in. If you want to come back and do time intensive work later on, that is great, but don't get derailed by making your work too big.

For me, I both paint and do digital work. Painting in gouache is okay if the cards are small, about postcard size. Painting on my iPad is even faster. Collaging on my computer is also really efficient for me. Decide on your approach. Make sure you have all the tools, brushes, glue, or whatever you might need ready now. Do your best to keep it always stocked and ready.

If you don't have a photo editing software you are comfortable with already, do a quick search for what is current, affordable, and works on your kind of computer, smart phone, or tablet. You may also be able to find editing software tutorials through the product's manufacturer or on YouTube. This kind of stuff has become easy and affordable, so don't be deterred.

Where can I find images?

I am a big fan of not stealing from artists, even if it is for private use. What you do is completely your choice. The simplest way to be on the right side of this is to go online to Creative Commons Search. They have a search engine that will allow you to search Google, Flickr, and other places for free-to-use images by checking off the "free to modify" and "use commercially" boxes.

Of course, you can also photograph your own world, too, which might help get more of your magick into the deck.

Photography

If you are going to make physical art – collage, painting, macramé, etc. – you need to plan out how you will photograph or scan the pieces. Start thinking about this now. If you need ideas, Google will be happy to help. Test your plan before the end. With the right lighting, an iPhone can do this, but it requires set up, lights, and practice. Avoid getting to the end and realizing you can't get as good an image as you like. You can always hire a photographer, too.

If you are going to use a computer to create your art, or just to add titles or borders, please go check out the "file set up" in the appendix section.

Making the art

If you are making physical art, you can always work bigger than the size at which you plan to print. Take care that your art is multiplied evenly. If you want to print a 2 x 4 inch card, you can work at 4 x 8 inches, but if it is not evenly scaled up, you will run into serious issues later on. Your work won't fit proportionally to the final cut, and it will look odd. Seriously, while this sounds straightforward, it is easy to make mistakes – especially if we start getting into fractions. Test to make sure you have it right.

Titles or numbers?

If you want to have titles on your cards, you will need to plan on how you will include them. Will they be added after? On top of the artwork? Or as part of the border? They can certainly be added to the final art going to print, but don't forget they might adjust your composition. The same holds true for numbers on your card. Think about it now.

Do you want a full deck?

Keeping in mind that many full decks take years to make. This process focuses on the Majors or Trump cards only. Consider making a simple set of numbered and court cards to round it out. If you are using a company that also prints playing cards, they may have art you can use too.

I am happy to help

I love guiding people through this process. Whether you hit a sticking point and just want a one-off session, or would like to work with me around every step of the process, I am available. We can work either in person or by Skype from anywhere. Drop me an email or head over to thehermitslamp.com/tarotofyou/

The Facebook Group

You are also invited to join the people doing this work on Facebook by friending me there and sending me a message. Please respect the people who are there. We are all grown ups here, so I know we can be polite, kind, and supportive with each other. The group is monitored to make sure it is a safe place to share.

The Fool

Day 1 - Opening to Imagery

Draw a card and invoke your synchronicity. (Refer to the instructions in the "Synchronistic Whatchamacallit" section of the Introduction). **Write down the card you drew.**

Roll your die once for each of the lists below. (The number will tell you which of the options to include on your card. For example, roll a 1 for question 1, and your biggest fear on the card is a gap. Roll a 6, and it is the open road.)

What are you most afraid of?
1. A gap
2. A cliff
3. A dragon
4. Crowds
5. Spiders
6. An open road

Who is with the Fool?
1. Friend
2. Foe
3. Pet
4. Acolyte
5. No one
6. Spirit

What is in the bag?
1. The eternal self
2. Gold
3. Lunch
4. Books
5. What bag?
6. Fancy clothes

As you work through this card, anytime you read "three elements" on another day's work, think back to these three questions and what the die chose for them.

Other elements you might consider including:

Foliage, butterflies, birds, etc.

Find, sketch, or write out as many possibilities for each as you can. Make sure to leave enough time to do this for all three ideas.

Day 2 - Putting It in Perspective

Before reading today's work (below), please take a moment to write down any synchronous message(s) or cue(s) you have received as a result of the card you drew yesterday.

*****

A big feature in many modern decks is the idea that the Fool is leaping off of something into the unknown. In older decks, the Fool is setting off on a journey with the unknown more implied than explicitly shown. The unknown represents both the goal and the problem. We can never fully know what getting to our goal will be like or the details of the path to get there.

The Fool is also almost always shown with somebody or something following them. Whether it is a jolly-looking white puppy or a more sinister-looking beast clawing at them, they are rarely alone. I often think of this companion as being the reason they left their house. On top of the conscious reason for leaving, this beastie also stands for the unconscious motivation too.

Depending on who you ask about what is in the Fool's bag, you will get many different answers. I like to think of it as containing the things they already contain but do not understand about themselves, yet. In the bag are strength, wisdom, perseverance, laughter, and other psychological and emotional tools that their journey will bring out in them.

Looking back on your list from yesterday, your synchronistic cue, and reading my comments today, sort through your imagery and write some ideas about how they relate to your life. If you think of a better image or symbol, make a note or add it to your collection.

Day 3 - Working the Title

The Fool is a concept that has lots of negative connotations in modern language.

1. What does it mean to be foolish?
2. What is the best thing about it?
3. What is the worst?
4. How are outsiders welcomed?
5. How are they ostracized?

Look back over what you just wrote and note any words that stand out. Explore what other words you might use for this card. Grab a thesaurus if you want and explore other words that might cover the spectrum of ideas in this card more clearly for you. Of course, you can keep the traditional title if you like, too.

Day 4 - Exploring Further

The three elements we have been talking about all work together to create this card. The Fool is not just the person shown in the card, but a synthesis of all three parts working together. Conscious, unconscious, and potential, all working together to create a life. Answer the following questions and dig into how the parts relate for you.

> The Fool's "Three Elements" are:
>
> What's in the Fool's path?
> Who is with the Fool?
> What is in the bag?

1. How does your unconscious motivate you?
2. How do others / the world impact your journey?
3. What obstacles do you avoid looking at?
4. What makes you so uncomfortable that you laugh at it?
5. When do you laugh the most?

When answering each of the questions for today, try to frame them in relationship to the three elements of the Fool from Day 1.

Day 5 - Embodiment

Do the following. Do not worry. No one can see you, so just go for it!

Set a timer for eight minutes. Start chanting

> **"I am perfect. I know nothing.**
> **I am nothing. I am the Fool."**

Just let it all fall into jumbles. If your tongue slips, then repeat the slip. If you make sounds, repeat them. Allow it to flow into blabbering.

When the timer sounds, make a note of whatever came up. How did the spirit of the Fool show you its nature during this time? See if anything needs to be added to your card from this exploration.

Without thinking, write down how the Fool is dressed.

If you need to gather more images, do so once you are done writing.

Day 6 - Looking at Elements

Review your images, words, and notes from this week's work. For each of the three elements, choose what you like most and least and explore how to include both in the card.

For example, I might like the idea of my childhood dog, Luke, to be with me in the card. A symbol of fun and free times exploring in nature. I rolled *foe* on the first day, and in my journaling realized how bullies have encouraged me to go on a journey of self-discovery over the years. Of course, the idea of putting bullies on my card is not one I like very much, but it is an important part of my story. I could include something in the background to represent this idea, like an outline of the public school I went to, or the place I lived, and also have my dog on the card with me. I could also think about the times with Luke and what might be a memory around him that includes both ideas. Like the time he dragged me, because my hand was caught in the leash, while he chased after a squirrel.

I also rolled that gold was in the bag, and that there should be a dragon on the card. I will design my Fool to be stepping over a dragon that is sleeping. The gold remains hidden in my design, since it is in the bag, but knowing that dragons like gold, it adds another layer to the card.

Day 7 - Combining the Elements

Put it all together. Hopefully, you have a good idea of what is in and out of the card, now. Remember that including the three elements in your card in some way will help solidify its meaning. The Fool's three elements are: *What are you afraid of? Who is with you? What is in the bag?* This is the day to create your card.

Now is the time to check your work

Once you have made your first card, double-check your setup is correct. If you are photographing your physical art, don't wait for all the cards to be done. Test this one now. If your work is digital, test that it is set to the right specifications. If you are printing it at a local copy shop, run a test image. If you are using an online service, upload a copy and make sure it fits correctly in the template. It could be a pain to remake this card, but it will be heartbreaking to finish the whole deck and find that you have 22 cards to redo.

The Magician

Day 1 - Opening to Imagery

Draw a card and invoke your synchronicity. (Refer to the instructions in the "Synchronistic Whatchamacallit" section of the introduction). Write down the card you drew.

Roll your die once for each of the lists below. (The number will tell you which of the options to include on your card.)

Who is the Magician performing for?
1. Themselves
2. Spirit
3. A cheering crowd
4. A jeering crowd
5. Their parents
6. Children

What must the Magician have on their table?
1. A wand, a cup, a knife, and a disk.
2. A game of chance
3. Crystal(s)
4. A computer
5. A spirit
6. An ape

(You can add other things too that you choose, but do include what comes up here in your process.)

What does the Magician wear?
1. Nothing
2. A robe
3. Yoga clothes
4. Traditional clothes
5. Black tie
6. Casual wear

As you work through this card, anytime you read "three elements" on another day's work, think back to these three questions and what the die chose for them.

Other elements you might consider including:

What posture is the Magician taking? Are they in nature, on a street corner, in a temple, or floating in the cosmic void?

Find, sketch, or write out as many ideas for each as you can. Make sure to leave enough time to do this for all three ideas.

Day 2 - Putting It in Perspective

Before reading today's work (below), please take a moment to write down any synchronous message(s) or cue(s) you have received as a result of the card you drew yesterday.

*****

The Magician is one of the most iconic cards in the deck. Wielding their wand and often wearing a fancy hat, they command attention and the power of the universe. In this card, at least in contemporary interpretations, all the elements work together to allow their power to flow. The Magician balances in the duality between truth, through their connection to spirit, and illusion, through their performance.

The Magician is always focused on a goal. Nothing about their actions is ever random or haphazard. Every gesture is deliberate. However, the Magician is also always reacting in relationship to their surroundings. They are watching their audience and adjusting their delivery to match the reactions they see. In that way, their surroundings and who they are performing for changes their actions and possibly even changes them over time. What is truthful and what is illusion?

The Magician uses the tools in front of them to achieve their goal. The tools also provide insight into how the Magician ticks. The interplay of the items represents the ways in which the internal life of the Magician works. When they are balanced, things go well and the Magician is more effective. When these elements are out of balance, the Magician might not be successful. What in your life and self are the important mechanisms of your power?

How we dress is a clear signifier of who we want to be in the world. The Magician has been shown in many kinds of attire throughout their history. Of course, these outfits had specific meanings in their time, but they have also become significant in other ways over time. The hat shown in the Marseille deck may have been in fashion in its time, but is now reminiscent of the infinity sign and connection to spirit. Nudity, for example, may be a symbol of sexuality, innocence, or a connection with nature.

Looking back on your list from yesterday, your synchronistic cue, and reading my comments today, sort through your imagery and write some ideas about how they relate to your life. If you think of a better image or symbol, make a note or add it to your collection.

Day 3 - Working the Title

The Magician conveys a duality of illusion and power. The ideas of both stage magick and ceremony are found in this card. In some ways, the older title of "The Juggler" is more satisfying to me, personally. It conveys the idea of movement and balance that pushes the bounds of what we think is possible. As a practice, juggling balances both sides of the mind.

1. What do you associate with the Magician?
2. What are five words that come to mind when you think about magick?
3. What role models can you think of for this card?
4. What performances feel powerful and true?
5. What performances feel illusionary and insincere?

Look back over what you just wrote and note any words that stand out. Explore what other words you might use for this card. Grab a thesaurus if you want and explore other words that might cover the spectrum of ideas in this card more clearly for you. Of course, you can keep the traditional title if you like, too.

Day 4 - Exploring Further

The three elements we have been talking about all work together to create this card. The Magician is the centre of connection, the audience and the performance. The items that must be with them represent their inner power. Those people

> The Magician's "Three Elements" are:
>
> Who are they performing for?
> What must be on the table?
> What does the Magician wear?

they perform for are the audience. Their attire speaks to the nature of their performance. We can go further and tie these to other ideas about your way of being in the world by exploring the following questions. Please look at these questions, both in the now and as part of a big picture of the themes in your life.

1. How do you feel about whom you are performing for?
2. Who have you felt inclined to perform for in the past?
3. How do you connect to your inner power?
4. What do you think about using illusion to achieve your goals?
5. What is spirit calling on you to share with a group or the world?
6. How do you feel about standing in front of other people?

When answering each of the questions for today, try to frame them in relationship to the three elements of the Magician from Day 1.

Day 5 – Embodiment

Do the following. Do not worry. No one can see you, so just go for it!

Set a timer for eight minutes. Start chanting,

> **"I am perfect. I know everything.
> I control what happens."**

Just let it all fall into jumbles. If your tongue slips, then repeat the slip. If you make sounds, repeat them. Allow it to flow into blabbering.

When the timer sounds, make a note of whatever came up. How did the spirit of the Magician show you its nature during this time? See if anything needs to be added to your card from this exploration.

Without thinking, write down the gesture the Magician appeared to be making.

If you need to gather more images, do so once you are done writing.

Day 6 - Looking at Elements

Review your images, words, and notes from this week's work. For each of the three elements, choose what you like most and least and explore how to include both in the card.

The Magician from my Tarot Waiting to Happen deck

For example, I might be performing for parents. In thinking about specific people in my life, it is important to be clear if I am talking about my current relationship, the story of my history with them, or a specific event. In regards to the Magician, my story is one of seeking to not step into the role of performing for anyone – including my family. So I might chose to show a parent looking the other way to include this notion of looking not to act in relationship to them.

Do not get caught up in recreating the imagery you are accustomed to seeing. On the left, I have included my Magician from my first deck, *Tarot Waiting to Happen*.

Day 7 - Combining the Elements

Put it all together. Hopefully, you have a good idea of what is in and out of the card, now. Remember that including the three elements in your card in some way will help solidify its meaning. The Magician's three elements are: *Who are you performing for? What must be on the table? What does the Magician wear?* This is the day to create your card.

The High Priestess

Day 1 – Opening to Imagery

Draw a card and invoke your synchronicity. (Refer to the instructions in the "Synchronistic Whatchamacallit" section of the Introduction). Write down the card you drew.

Roll your die once for each of the lists below. (The number will tell you which of the options to include on your card.)

What is around them?
1. Two pillars
2. Trees
3. A temple
4. The sea
5. The solar system
6. Nothing

What is the High Priestess holding?
1. A book
2. A crystal
3. A sceptre
4. Light
5. A flower
6. A feather

What secret does she keep?
1. Knowledge of the Goddess
2. The power of nature
3. The language of birds
4. Mysteries of reincarnation
5. The word of God
6. Psychic powers

As you work through this card, anytime you read "three elements" on another day's work, think back to these three questions and what the die chose for them.

Other elements you might consider including:

What is on her head? What other symbols does she wear, or can be found in the space? Where is she looking? At us? Into the unknown? Eyes closed in meditation?

Find, sketch, or write out as many possibilities for each as you can. Make sure to leave enough time to do this for all three ideas.

Day 2 – Putting It in Perspective

Before reading today's work (below), please take a moment to write down any synchronous message(s) or cue(s) you have received as a result of the card you drew yesterday.

*****

The Priestess is one of the most popular cards in the deck. She speaks of a certain kind of female power – mysterious and practical at the same time. In some decks she is known as the Popess, and is often seen as the counterpart to the Hierophant/Pope card.

In the Rider Waite Smith deck, she is shown with a black pillar on one side and a white pillar on the other. This references things like masonry, the temple of Solomon, and the tree of life in the Qabala. In the Thoth deck, she is connected to the flow of space and time, and at her feet are platonic crystals, revealing the pure world of archetypes. Both sets of symbols speak to divine connection between the order of the universe and the power that this card embodies.

Most depictions of this card show her holding a book or scroll of holy texts. Perhaps it is Rumi's poetry, the Tao Te Ching, a Bible, or something else, but always at its heart is a revelation of spiritual truth. The thing about revealed or received teachings is that they require scrutiny and contemplation to digest. They are obscure, esoteric, and complex because the spiritual truths of life can only be pointed at and never fully communicated in language.

The Priestess understands the mysteries and secrets that empower, and is trusted to keep them secret. Beginners want everything revealed to them at the start. Yet even when they hear the most profound mysteries, they often cannot benefit from them because they lack the experience that is required to interpret the mysteries correctly. In many ways, the further one journeys on their path, the more one knows that cannot be shared. So the Priestess serves her mysteries and keeps them sacred and secret.

Day 3 - Working the Title

The Priestess conveys a certain kind of power – especially in pagan circles – that is attainable. The Popess possesses a kind of power that must be given by spirit and conferred by the Church. This card also has ties with being an elder, a wise woman, a crone, and so on.

1. What powerful female role models do you admire?
2. Do you think anyone can attain this card's level of wisdom?
3. How does feminine power differ from male power?
4. Is the position shown in this card earned or destined?
5. How does tradition play a role in intuitive growth?

Look back over what you just wrote and note any words that stand out. Explore what other words you might use for this card. Grab a thesaurus if you want and explore other words that might cover the spectrum of ideas in this card more clearly for you. Of course, you can keep the traditional title if you like, too.

Day 4 - Exploring Further

The three elements we have been talking about all work together to create this card. The Priestess manifests their power through her place in the material world, her source of power that she holds a symbol of, and what she keeps secret. Together, these three elements combine to create a presence in the world that is both obvious and hidden at the same time. Unlike the Magician, whose silence is part of the act, the Priestess's secrecy preserves the sacredness of her position and that which she serves.

> The Priestess's "Three Elements" are:
>
> What is around them?
> What are they holding?
> What secret do they keep?

1. How do you feel about the place in which you find your spirituality?
2. What are the roots of your knowing?
3. What is public about your spirituality?
4. What is private about it?
5. In the balance between speech and silence, how do you know when to keep things secret?
6. What do you think/feel about channeled messages?
7. What kind of service, if any, do you feel drawn to?

When answering each of the questions for today, try to frame them in relationship to the three elements of the Priestess from Day 1.

Day 5 - Embodiment

Do the following. Do not worry. No one can see you, so just go for it!

Set a timer for eight minutes. Start chanting,

"In silence I know. From knowing I connect. From connection I serve."

Just let it all fall into jumbles. If your tongue slips, then repeat the slip. If you make sounds, repeat them. Allow it to flow into blabbering.

When the timer sounds, make a note of whatever came up. How did the spirit of the Priestess show you its nature during this time? See if anything needs to be added to your card from this exploration.

Without thinking, write down the gesture the Priestess appeared to be making.

If you need to gather more images, do so once you are done writing.

Day 6 - Looking at Elements

Review your images, words, and notes from this week's work. For each of the three elements, choose what you like most and least and explore how to include both in the card.

Having rolled that the High Priestess keeps a secret, I noticed that I have a few contexts in which I serve where secrecy and privacy are important. The obvious and first one is through my store, where I do readings. It defines many things about my relationship with the people who come for guidance. It is public, yet it limits their access to me personally. It requires money and only happens in specific ways. I keep few secrets in this context. Conversely, in my role as a priest I am harder to find. It is more private, and the relationships with those with whom I work are more personal and deeply connected to my personal life. My service to the spirits with which I work fuels both of the roles above. Both roles might need to be shown in my card, or perhaps one is only alluded to.

I also rolled a feather and the sea, both being very strong symbols of how I work spiritually. The sea itself is a source of mystery – no one knows what lies at the bottom of it. Mystery, like the depth of the sea, is a cornerstone of how I think about reading cards. At a certain point, we can only know what comes to the surface. Feathers allow birds to fly and be seen as beings that carry messages from the spirit world to this one. I feel a deep affinity with a variety of birds, but especially the vulture that is often associated with spiritual powers like the ones I work with at my shop. So I'll include a vulture feather in the design.

Day 7 - Combining the Elements

Put it all together. Hopefully, you have a good idea of what is in and out of the card, now. Remember that including the three elements in your card in some way will help solidify its meaning. The Priestess's three elements are: *What is around them? What are they holding? What secret do they keep?* This is the day to create your card.

The Empress

Day 1 - Opening to Imagery

Draw a card and invoke your synchronicity. (Refer to the instructions in the "Synchronistic Whatchamacallit" section of the Introduction). Write down the card you drew.

Roll your die once for each of the lists below. (The number will tell you which of the options to include on your card.)

What are they pregnant with?
1. A child
2. Love
3. Nature
4. Healing
5. Service
6. Possibility

Where in nature is the Empress sitting?
1. A lake
2. A river
3. An ocean
4. A farm
5. A mountain
6. A forest

What or whom does she serve?
1. Compassion
2. The world
3. Children
4. The wounded
5. The sick
6. Artists

As you work through this card, anytime you read "three elements" on another day's work, think back to these three questions and what the die chose for them.

Other elements you might consider including:

Are there other beings with her? Birds, butterflies, or something else? Is she pregnant? What is she sitting on? Or is she standing?

Find, sketch, or write out as many possibilities for each as you can. Make sure to leave enough time to do this for all three ideas.

Day 2 – Putting It in Perspective

Before reading today's work (below), please take a moment to write down any synchronous message(s) or cue(s) you have received as a result of the card you drew yesterday.

*****

The Empress is the kinder, gentler, maternal energy of the tarot. This card is all loving, all giving, and always nurturing. Of course, this card is also an archetype and not a human being. As we journey through these cards, it becomes more and more important to be mindful not to over identify with any specific card. The kind of lush summer day this card metaphorically speaks of cannot go on forever. As a source of nurture and support, though, she can always be there for us.

The Empress represents *fecundity*. Whether or not she is actually pregnant, her energy encourages us to conceive and give birth to things. This may be art, a child, or some other project. We could put it another way and say that she is the muse of the world. Driving the birds to sing. Urging the salmon to swim upstream to reproduce. Inspiring the words of poets since the dawn of time.

"Fecundity"

The quality of being fecund; capacity, especially in female animals, of producing young in great numbers.

Every place in nature has its own energy or vibe. The calm of a quiet lake is different from, but related to, the power of the sea, which is often far more active. A grassy field might inspire a nap, while the shady depths of a forest will reveal other secrets to us. The variety of settings in which we find the Empress show both the ways in which she manifests and where her power comes from.

Service is an interesting concept to wrap your head around. What do I have to give, to whom, and under what conditions? How do I balance my needs against the needs of those I serve? At work, life may be more clearly defined – I serve during these hours. For parents, that line is almost impossible to hold – when the kids are sick you are on call 24/7. In any role where we seek to help, we must find these lines and negotiate the right balance between doing enough – being of service – and doing too much – sacrificing ourselves to others' needs.

Day 3 - Working the Title

The Empress is, as we have talked about, a card of love, compassion, and nurturing. Whether we call her the muse, the gardener, the mother, fertility, or love, she represents all of these and more.

1. What does nurture look like in the natural world?
2. Is there a moral imperative to help or be of service?
3. How does nature connect to spirituality?
4. What might make someone unworthy of nurturing?
5. Is gender important to the ideas in this card?

Look back over what you just wrote and note any words that stand out. Explore what other words you might use for this card. Grab a thesaurus if you want and explore other words that might cover the spectrum of ideas in this card more clearly for you. Of course, you can keep the traditional title if you like, too.

Day 4 - Exploring Further

The three elements we have been talking about all work together to create this card. The Empress both gives birth to the natural world and draws power from it. Certainly, she does so in service of something.

> The Empress's "Three Elements" are:
>
> What are they pregnant with?
> Where in nature are they?
> Who or what do they serve?

Often that idea is seen as an emblem on a shield, or banner, in the card. There is no easy distinction between where these three elements play out in this card. What came first? Her call to service? Her creation of nature? Or her ability to draw power from the world? It is chickens and eggs, all the way to infinity.

1. What would you like to birth into your life?
2. What holds you back from doing so?
3. When you are helping people, are they changing, or are you enabling them?
4. What helps you keep moving forward in hard times?
5. Where are the boundaries of your service to others?
6. How much do you help others?
7. How gracefully do you let others help you?
8. How can you help the world?
9. What holds you back?
10. How do you relate to nature?
11. Where do you feel most connected to the earth?

When answering each of the questions for today, try to frame them in relationship to the three elements of the Empress from Day 1.

Day 5 - Embodiment

Do the following. Do not worry. No one can see you, so just go for it!

Set a timer for eight minutes. Start chanting,

> **"Love makes the seed open. Love moves the heart. Love is what I serve."**

Just let it all fall into jumbles. If your tongue slips, then repeat the slip. If you make sounds, repeat them. Allow it to flow into blabbering.

When the timer sounds, make a note of whatever came up. How did the spirit of the Empress show you its nature during this time? See if anything needs to be added to your card from this exploration.

Without thinking, write down the gesture the Empress appeared to be making.

If you need to gather more images, do so once you are done writing.

Day 6 - Looking at Elements

Review your images, words, and notes from this week's work. For each of the three elements, choose what you like most and least and explore how to include both in the card.

I rolled service, a forest, and children.

While the High Priestess is also about service, the Empress represents the boundless nurture of love and creativity. She is less formal and usually not tied to any particular institution or structure. In the context of the elements in this card, I am giving birth to tools of truth – like this book. My power comes from my connection to spirits and their representatives in the world – other priests, birds, and plants. I have a place in the ravine by my store that is a power spot to me. It is always healing to be there. Simply put, I serve the Orisha. I could also say I serve the forces of truth that seek to awaken and enlighten humanity.

In my life, I serve without limit in very few contexts. I have two children to whom I give everything when they need it. I serve the spirits in my care also.

Day 7 - Combining the Elements

Put it all together. Hopefully, you have a good idea of what is in and out of the card now. Remember that including the three elements in your card in some way will help solidify its meaning. The Empress's three elements are: *What are they pregnant with? Where in nature are they? Whom or what do they serve?* This is the day to create your card.

The Emperor

Day 1 - Opening to Imagery

Draw a card and invoke your synchronicity. (Refer to the instructions in the "Synchronistic Whatchamacallit" section of the Introduction). Write down the card you drew.

Roll your die once for each of the lists below. (The number will tell you which of the options to include on your card.)

What is the symbol of worldly power?
1. A pen
2. A sceptre
3. A crown
4. A sphere crowned with a cross
5. The look in your eyes
6. Your hands

What symbolizes the source of the Emperor's power?
1. A ram
2. A tiger
3. A tree
4. A mountain
5. A religious symbol
6. A sword

How do people relate to their leadership?
1. Happily
2. Begrudgingly
3. With fear
4. They don't
5. Seriously
6. Lazily

As you work through this card, anytime you read "three elements" on another day's work, think back to these three questions and what the die chose for them.

Other elements you might consider including:

The throne, crown, and other trappings are important to the Emperor. Where is the Emperor looking? At us, or to the left or right?

Find, sketch, or write out as many possibilities for each as you can. Make sure to leave enough time to do this for all three ideas.

Day 2 - Putting It in Perspective

Before reading today's work (below), please take a moment to write down any synchronous message(s) or cue(s) you have received as a result of the card you drew yesterday.

*****

The Emperor represents the idea of worldly power and leadership. This kind of power is often a balancing act. Too much fire, and things fall apart. Too much overreaching, and the kingdom does not grow. Of course, not enough fire and nothing happens at all. In the middle, we find the Emperor. On their throne, directing the show. Often, the card also indicates something about what the Emperor themself needs in order to be renewed for the next day's efforts.

It is of note that the Emperor carries a symbol of their power. Though many Emperors might have won their title in combat, they don't carry a weapon. They might cudgel someone with their sceptre, but it is an unlikely weapon and not designed for combat. What they carry is in fact more powerful than a weapon. It is the authority to tell others to fight or act on their behalf. To rise from the throne in order to fight would actually undermine their power.

To be Emperor is to be divinely appointed to the throne. The Emperor stands as a worldly emissary of some greater power. Is it God? Wisdom? Truth? In many ways, the source of the Emperor's power is ineffable – it can only be indicated by something else. A lion for bravery and justness. An eagle for wisdom and perspective. These trappings convey a lot of things about the nature, character, and way of walking in the world that a particular Emperor might embody.

The Emperor, of course, is also a leader. Their job is to guide their kingdom to better times. The way in which they rule is in direct relationship to how people feel about them. I had a pair of landlords a while back that showed two very opposite faces to the situation. The one was always kind, humble, polite, and easygoing. The other a tyrant who would fight, argue, and always do what they wanted. Now, in dealing with the one, I was pretty happy and things went well. With the other, I really disliked them and struggled with myself to be able to wish them well.

Day 3 - Working the Title

The Emperor is about power, authority, governance, and structure. They can be a parental figure, too. In general the way in which we relate to this figure goes to our childhood and the way authority treated us then.

1. Is divine authority valid?
2. What does the Emperor owe those he rules?
3. How does patriarchy fit into this card?
4. Is rulership tied to wisdom, might, or something else?
5. What does it mean that the Emperor sits back while others serve, work, and fight for them?

Look back over what you just wrote and note any words that stand out. Explore what other words you might use for this card. Grab a thesaurus if you want and explore other words that might cover the spectrum of ideas in this card more clearly for you. Of course, you can keep the traditional title if you like, too.

Day 4 - Exploring Further

The three elements we have been talking about all work together to create this card. The Emperor sits in the balance amidst the

> The Emperor's "Three Elements" are:
>
> What is the symbol of worldly power?
> What symbolizes the source of the Emperor's power?
> How do people relate to their leadership?

source that granted his authority, his actions, or way of being as shown by the symbol of his power, and the people whom he leads. The interplay of these three could be in harmony or not. If one is not working, then things can really get out of hand. When we have these three things working well, there are few limits to what we can accomplish.

1. Are you comfortable in your life?
2. Are you serving your higher truth?
3. What about your showing your own power is working well?
4. What about your showing your own power is working poorly?
5. How do you gauge what you get as feedback from others?
6. Are you comfortable leading?
7. Do you question authority?
8. How do you feel about power?
9. Is justice an important idea in your life?
10. What do you believe is a worthy source of power?
11. How do you think people feel about your leadership/suggestions?

When answering each of the questions for today, try to frame them in relationship to the three elements of the Emperor from Day 1.

Day 5 - Embodiment

Do the following. Do not worry. No one can see you, so just go for it!

Set a timer for eight minutes. Start chanting,

"From spirit, to earth. From sky to sea. I govern all I see."

Just let it all fall into jumbles. If your tongue slips, then repeat the slip. If you make sounds, repeat them. Allow it to flow into blabbering.

When the timer sounds, make a note of whatever came up. How did the spirit of the Emperor show you its nature during this time? See if anything needs to be added to your card from this exploration.

Without thinking, write down the gesture the Emperor appeared to be making.

If you need to gather more images, do so once you are done writing.

Day 6 – Looking at Elements

The Emperor from my Tarot Waiting to Happen deck.

Review your images, words, and notes from this week's work. For each of the three elements, choose what you like most and least and explore how to include both in the card.

I am the Emperor of my shop. I don't wear a fancy hat, but I could, because it is mine to govern. The name of the shop and many other features suggest I serve tarot. This is not untrue. Really, I serve a mystery, but "tarot" is as good a word or symbol for it as anything else. My territory ends at the door. So when folks leave it is no longer my place to offer advice. Same holds true when I leave. All the spirits I work with have symbolic presences in the reading room. They convey the message of the other side, where I get my information from. It matters to me because, in my context, my "rule" is reliant on clients, in the bigger sense. However, in the session, my rule is without question. It is my job to take the person through a process and to stay in control, even if they don't. Although in the moment of the reading people may even hate me, in time, people usually feel good about my guidance. Of course, some don't get there right away, and maybe some never do. Regardless of their feelings or reactions, I must hold my course.

Day 7 - Combining the Elements

Put it all together. Hopefully, you have a good idea of what is in and out of the card now. Remember that including the three elements in your card in some way will help solidify its meaning. The Emperor's three elements are: *What is your symbol of worldly power? What symbolizes the source of your power? How do people relate to your leadership?* This is the day to create your card.

The Hierophant

Day 1 - Opening to Imagery

Draw a card and invoke your synchronicity. (Refer to the instructions in the "Synchronistic Whatchamacallit" section of the Introduction). Write down the card you drew.

Roll your die once for each of the lists below. (The number will tell you which of the options to include on your card.)

What is the Hierophant holding?
1. A rubber chicken
2. A trident
3. A shepherd's crook
4. A key
5. A mirror
6. A sheaf of wheat

Who are the people in front of the Hierophant?
1. The character with the Fool
2. The audience from the Magician
3. Sinners
4. Lost souls
5. The Sun and Moon
6. Apostles

What is the Hierophant revealing?
 1. Truth
 2. Illusions
 3. Science
 4. Nothing
 5. Reality
 6. The Way

As you work through this card, anytime you read "three elements" on another day's work, think back to these three questions and what the die chose for them.

Other elements you might consider including:

Where are they? A church, secret grove, temple, or elsewhere? What clothing is symbolic of wisdom to you? What institutions are wise?

Find, sketch, or write out as many possibilities for each as you can. Make sure to leave enough time to do this for all three ideas.

Day 2 - Putting It in Perspective

Before reading today's work (below), please take a moment to write down any synchronous message(s) or cue(s) you have received as a result of the card you drew yesterday.

*****

The word Hierophant is often translated as "the revealer of the sacred." This card is about the people and things that form a bridge between us and something else. The priest mediates and creates a bridge to God for us. Institutions bridge the makers of law and policy, who run countries, and the people who need things from them.

The Hierophant often carries a staff or other symbol of their connection and authority. The symbol itself shows us about the structure that the Hierophant is working for or is authorized by. Is it stern? Authoritarian? Humorous? Compassionate? We can tell a lot from this symbol. Possibly we can even see what this character thinks about humanity. Do we need guidance? Are we sheep? Are they giving us power, or expecting us to flock to their power?

Who we attract says a lot about us. They say the five people you spend the most time with can reveal who you are. Often, the people who are around us are there because they are getting something from us. That can be a great thing if they want love and support. Or it can be a problem if they only like us at payday.

As I said, the Hierophant reveals things. Have you experienced a moment when another person showed you something about yourself, or the universe that has blown your mind? My kids blow my mind all the time, as do my clients. Understanding the nature of what we know, how it can help people, and when to reveal it, is crucial to both being helpful and respecting our sacred knowledge.

Day 3 - Working the Title

The Hierophant is an initiator, a bridge, a mentor, guide, guru, holy person, and much more. This is one of the cards that can stand in for fatherhood in a reading.

1. What can a spiritually advanced person pass on to others?
2. Is self-guiding possible?
3. What makes a person able to take on this role?
4. What could make a person lose their spiritual power?
5. Is there a difference between spirituality and religion?
6. What is promised by the combination of the Hierophant's appearance, surroundings, and other elements?

Look back over what you just wrote and note any words that stand out. Explore what other words you might use for this card. Grab a thesaurus if you want and explore other words that might cover the spectrum of ideas in this card more clearly for you. Of course, you can keep the traditional title if you like, too.

Day 4 - Exploring Further

The three elements we have been talking about all work together to create this card. The Hierophant is given the wisdom that they then bring into the world by some authority. They clothe themselves

> The Hierophant's "Three Elements" are:
>
> What are they is holding?
> Who is in front of them?
> What are they revealing?

in symbols of the wisdom they possess. Their presentation then attracts people to whom they are able to reveal their wisdom.

1. What do you know?
2. How do you feel about being in a place of authority?
3. When do people expect something untrue from you?
4. What sacred authority would you, or do you, respect?
5. How is your relationship to your inner father?
6. In what ways are you a guide?
7. Who do you attract?
8. Do you feel you are wise?
9. Where do you go looking for wisdom?
10. What symbols draw you?
11. What is the biggest lesson you are working on in this life?

When answering each of the questions for today, try to frame them in relationship to the three elements of The Hierophant from Day 1.

Day 5 - Embodiment

Do the following. Do not worry. No one can see you, so just go for it!

Set a timer for eight minutes. Start chanting

"I open myself to wisdom so I may open wide the world to it, too."

Just let it all fall into jumbles. If your tongue slips, then repeat the slip. If you make sounds, repeat them. Allow it to flow into blabbering.

When the timer sounds, make a note of whatever came up. How did the spirit of the Hierophant show you its nature during this time? See if anything needs to be added to your card from this exploration.

Without thinking, write down the gesture the Hierophant appeared to be making.

If you need to gather more images, do so once you are done writing.

Day 6 - Looking at Elements

Review your images, words, and notes from this week's work. For each of the three elements, choose what you like most and least and explore how to include both in the card.

I used to feel like I needed a catchy title or symbol to draw the right people to my business. However, I never struck upon one. Instead, I found that the symbol for my store does the trick. Eight points for Mercury, god of communication; Solar, looking for the light of the sun, the visible face of God; the Hermit's lamp, for the act of searching and guiding, but always being true to what I have found by looking inside. People are drawn in all the time and say, "I saw your logo and just had to come in." The choice of the Hermit implies directly that I will not take followers or be a guru. Instead, I will help people light their lanterns and send them on their way. The knowing informs the symbols, which then invites the people with whom my mysteries are most likely to resonate.

Day 7 - Combining the Elements

Put it all together. Hopefully, you have a good idea of what is in and out of the card now. Remember that including the three elements in your card in some way will help solidify its meaning. The Hermit's three elements are: *What he is holding? Who is in front of them? What are they revealing?* This is the day to create your card.

The Lovers

Day 1 - Opening to Imagery

Draw a card and invoke your synchronicity. (Refer to the instructions in the "Synchronistic Whatchamacallit" section of the Introduction). Write down the card you drew.

Roll your die once for each of the lists below. (The number will tell you which of the options to include on your card.)

What is the central figure choosing between?
1. Love and hate
2. Two lovers
3. Family and love
4. Truth and lies
5. Freedom and responsibility
6. No choice. They are taking both.

Who, or what is above the scene?
1. Cupid
2. Guardian angel
3. The Sun
4. The Hermit
5. The shadow
6. A bird

What is the central character looking for?
1. Love
2. Sex
3. Power
4. Money
5. Wisdom
6. Healing

As you work through this card, anytime you read "three elements" on another day's work, think back to these three questions and what the die chose for them.

Other elements you might consider including:

Other characters and animals? Natural elements in the background, or are they inside?

Find, sketch, or write out as many possibilities for each as you can. Make sure to leave enough time to do this for all three ideas.

Day 2 - Putting It in Perspective

Before reading today's work (below), please take a moment to write down any synchronous message(s) or cue(s) you have received as a result of the card you drew yesterday.

*****

The Lovers is a complicated card that many modern interpretations greatly simplify. It may be about love. However, it may also be about the various parts within the person asking the question. Conscious, unconscious, and superconscious, all working together or fighting for control. It can tell the story of Cain and Abel, according to Crowley, and in some decks tells of the saving of Andromeda from the Kraken by Perseus. So certainly there is something deeper than a roll in the hay going on with this card.

First, we need to consider the choice. Are we choosing the hero's path, or a mundane one? Are we looking for our soul mate, or someone to spend the night with? Any option can be fine – there is no judgment required – but being unclear about what you are choosing between can cause a lot of problems.

Second, we need to determine what the inspiring or guiding influence is on this scene? Cupid may move us in one way, while the Hierophant may counsel something entirely different. We like to think we are free to choose what we want, but the influence in the second role implies we are being guided towards something specific by a force that we are not in control of. Being unattached to the outcomes of life is what allows us to be free.

Finally, people often set out after something specific and then lose track of it, as life presents them with options. So we can decide that we want a career that shines for decades to come, but then love might encourage us to not take that job in another country, and our course changes. This may or may not be a problem. It might be the best choice to put love first. Of course, the opposite might be true, too.

Day 3 - Working the Title

The Lovers is about finding our relationships in the world. In many ways, it is about taking what we have been given, learned, or been imprinted with from the Priestess, Empress, Emperor, and Hierophant, and trying to find our way into the world.

1. Is love real?
2. Can we trust what we know?
3. Can we know what is in another person's heart or mind?
4. How does the unconscious factor in to this card?
5. Can we become clear about the influence of others in our lives?

Look back over what you just wrote and note any words that stand out. Explore what other words you might use for this card. Grab a thesaurus if you want and explore other words that might cover the spectrum of ideas in this card more clearly for you. Of course, you can keep the traditional title if you like, too.

Day 4 - Exploring Further

The three elements we have been talking about all work together to create this card. The Lovers card is made up of the options in front of the Lover (central figure), what is above them pushing them forward, and what they set out looking for in the beginning. Among these options, the Lover exerts their free will.

> The Lovers's "Three Elements" are:
>
> What are they choosing between?
> Who is above them?
> What is the central person looking for?

1. Who motivates you?
2. What do you desire?
3. What do you wish the options in front of you were?
4. How free do you feel?
5. Has inspiration pierced your heart?
6. Who inspires the choices you are making (even if it is a rejection)?
7. Do you feel you need rescuing?
8. Are you the hero of your life?
9. Do you like the options in front of you?
10. How close is your fantasy life to reality?
11. What choices are you putting off?

When answering each of the questions for today, try to frame them in relationship to the three elements of the Lovers from Day 1.

Day 5 - Embodiment

Do the following. Do not worry. No one can see you, so just go for it!

Set a timer for eight minutes. Start chanting

"I love myself. I choose myself. I choose to live as myself."

Just let it all fall into jumbles. If your tongue slips, then repeat the slip. If you make sounds, repeat them. Allow it to flow into blabbering.

When the timer sounds, make a note of whatever came up. How did the spirit of the Lovers show you its nature during this time? See if anything needs to be added to your card from this exploration.

Without thinking, write down what the Lover is wearing.

If you need to gather more images, do so once you are done writing.

Day 6 - Looking at Elements

Review your images, words, and notes from this week's work. For each of the three elements, choose what you like most and least and explore how to include both in the card.

The Lovers from my Tarot Waiting to Happen deck.

Ultimately, this card is all about what is going on inside of us. Though it points outward by making it look like a choice between two things, it is not really a fork in the road. It is about our authenticity or lack thereof. Are we aware of what is moving us and what we crave in relation to the choices we are making regularly? For me, there is a central idea of choosing to be "spiritual" that implies many aspects of my life. I don't fear judgement, but I do need to be conscious in my choices. My work comes out of my connection and closeness to spirit and requires attention and action to maintain. When I don't keep up my practices, my connection to spirit suffers. As does my ability to help clients. My practices keep me on the road and come from the higher spirits that walk with me.

So I might I seek wisdom, guided by my spirits, and choose between connection to spirit and worldly needs.

Day 7 - Combining the Elements

Put it all together. Hopefully, you have a good idea of what is in and out of the card now. Remember that including the three elements in your card in some way will help solidify its meaning. The Lovers' three elements are: *What are they choosing between? Who is above them? What is the central person looking for?* This is the day to create your card.

The Chariot

Day 1 - Opening to Imagery

Draw a card and invoke your synchronicity. (Refer to the instructions in the "Synchronistic Whatchamacallit" section of the Introduction). Write down the card you drew.

Roll your die once for each of the lists below. (The number will tell you which of the options to include on your card.)

What is pulling the Chariot?
1. Dogs
2. Horses
3. Hybrid creature (sphinx, hippogriff, etc.)
4. Dragons
5. Cars
6. Nothing

Where is the Charioteer going?
1. Earth
2. Heaven
3. To war
4. On holiday
5. To their destiny
6. On patrol

How is the Charioteer dressed?
1. In armour
2. Formally
3. In a uniform
4. As a priest
5. Like a Roman (toga)
6. Menacingly

As you work through this card, anytime you read "three elements" on another day's work, think back to these three questions and what the die chose for them.

Other elements you might consider including:

Can you see the Charioteer's face? What flag or emblem are they flying? Where are they looking? Is there anything in their hands?

Find, sketch, or write out as many possibilities for each as you can. Make sure to leave enough time to do this for all three ideas.

Day 2 - Putting It in Perspective

Before reading today's work (below), please take a moment to write down any synchronous message(s) or cue(s) you have received as a result of the card you drew yesterday.

*****

The Chariot goes. It is often associated with being on your path and heading out to do what you need to do. Some say this person is the Archangel Michael heading out to enforce God's will. Crowley suggests that it is God themselves concealed in the armour, and if we were to lift the visor, we would be destroyed by the glory of seeing God face-to-face. Who they are, where they are going, and why, determine a lot about this card. In all cases, though, we need to acknowledge they are on the right track.

The animals that pull the chariot tell us about the challenge/mastery in this card. Whatever the animal symbolizes in life must be controlled, harnessed, and directed in order to make progress. As a symbol, an ox would symbolize work and grounding. Generally, there are two animals here, which also speaks to the nature of the world as being embedded in duality. On the earth, everything is polarized between good and bad, pleasure and pain, or conscious and unconscious. All these dualities are under control in this card.

When we see the Chariot, we often need to ask, "Where is the person going?" Maybe they are not even in motion yet. Once we know where they are going, we need to figure out how they can stay on track. If we are heading to something new or something old it makes a big difference to the way in which the experience will start and go. We cannot lose track of the fact that this card is, in its historical context, a martial one. The chariot was a weapon of war. Are you going to break with history or include it?

The way in which the Charioteer is dressed and standing tells us a lot about their approach to the world. The duality in this card reminds us to look at the various symbols as having two possible meanings. Armour conveys power and the need for protection. The appearance of confidence might be real or it might be a mask.

Day 3 - Working the Title

The Chariot certainly encourages us to clarity, balance, and action. When all three are working well, this card is like a rocket ship.

1. Is there a right road for each person?
2. How can we find our calling in life?
3. Is conflict required in life?
4. Are the dualities talked about inherent in life?
5. Can we move beyond duality?

Look back over what you just wrote and note any words that stand out. Explore what other words you might use for this card. Grab a thesaurus if you want and explore other words that might cover the spectrum of ideas in this card more clearly for you. Of course, you can keep the traditional title if you like, too.

Day 4 – Exploring Further

The three elements we have been talking about all work together to create this card. The Chariot is a combination of the work shown by the animals, a purpose shown by the destination, and a way of interacting with the world as implied by the attire the Charioteer wears.

> The Chariot's "Three Elements" are:
>
> What is pulling the Chariot?
> Where are they going?
> How are they dressed?

1. Where are you going?
2. Whose banner are you working under?
3. How in control of your animals are you?
4. How close are you to your goals?
5. Are you ready to fight?
6. How will you know when you have won?
7. Are you comfortable in your power?
8. Do you like where you are going?
9. Who is balancing all three elements well?
10. What keeps your animals working together?
11. How does it feel when you are doing something associated with your purpose?

When answering each of the questions for today, try to frame them in relationship to the three elements of the Chariot from Day 1.

Day 5 - Embodiment

Do the following. Do not worry. No one can see you, so just go for it!

Set a timer for eight minutes. Start chanting,

"Go with purpose, go with power, go find victory."

Just let it all fall into jumbles. If your tongue slips, then repeat the slip. If you make sounds, repeat them. Allow it to flow into blabbering.

When the timer sounds, make a note of whatever came up. How did the spirit of the Chariot show you its nature during this time? See if anything needs to be added to your card from this exploration.

Without thinking, write down the gesture the Charioteer appeared to be making.

If you need to gather more images, do so once you are done writing.

Day 6 - Looking at Elements

Review your images, words, and notes from this week's work. For each of the three elements, choose what you like most and least and explore how to include both in the card.

I am continually working to not fight or be at war. My martial approach is more and more like a tai chi master. Turn and deflect. This applies to myself as much as the world. My animals would have to be nimble – probably winged, too, so they can just go where they need to without too much fuss. My destination is tranquility – though I fly a banner of truth. That is the duality I work to balance. Speaking what is real and avoiding conflict that I don't want or need to be in. My attire would be something comfortable and unassuming. I don't like the idea of wearing tai chi robes, as it feels culturally inappropriate, but perhaps linen pants and shirt. Casual, with a lot of allowance for mobility.

Day 7 - Combining the Elements

Put it all together. Hopefully, you have a good idea of what is in and out of the card now. Remember that including the three elements in your card in some way will help solidify its meaning. The Chariot's three elements are: *What is pulling the Chariot? Where are they going? How are they dressed?* This is the day to create your card.

Justice

Day 1 - Opening to Imagery

Draw a card and invoke your synchronicity. (Refer to the instructions in the "Synchronistic Whatchamacallit" section of the Introduction). Write down the card you drew.

Roll your die once for each of the lists below. (The number will tell you which of the options to include on your card.)

What represents the balance?
1. A traditional set of scales
2. A teeter-totter
3. A calliper
4. An open hand
5. A feather
6. A flower

What is in the right hand of the figure?
1. A gavel
2. A sword
3. A gun
4. A book
5. A closed fist
6. A set of handcuffs

Where is the figure?
1. In a court room
2. In nature
3. On a mountain
4. At a rally
5. In an office
6. At a prison

As you work through this card, anytime you read "three elements" on another day's work, think back to these three questions and what the die chose for them.

Other elements you might consider including:

How is the figure dressed? Is anyone else there? If there is a balance scale, is anything in it? Are they blindfolded?

Find, sketch, or write out as many possibilities for each as you can. Make sure to leave enough time to do this for all three ideas.

Day 2 - Putting It in Perspective

Before reading today's work (below), please take a moment to write down any synchronous message(s) or cue(s) you have received as a result of the card you drew yesterday.

*****

The Justice card represents the rules of society and culture that work to prevent chaos. It is not the actual enforcement or writing of the rules, but the judging of whether they are being broken or not. Justice is often seen as being impartial. Crowley changed the name of this card to "Adjustment" to highlight the way in which balance is temporary – just try to stand on one foot for a while, and you'll see exactly what he means.

In one hand – usually the left hand of the figure – we often have a set of scales. This can speak to the act of judging, or weighing out, what is right and wrong. It can also speak to the motivation of this character. They seek to bring things into balance when they are out of balance. You don't go to court if your life is in harmony with the world and you are living a happy life.

It the right hand, we usually see a sword. We can read this symbol as representing the actual judgement or verdict, compared to the judging aspect shown in the scales. It can also speak to the idea of enforcement. Behave, or the sword will be pointed at you. Once this symbol is set in motion, you no longer have recourse. Mercy or severity will be handed down, and everyone involved will have to live with the verdict and its consequences.

Ideally, Justice could be found everywhere. In all the social encounters we go through, it would be wonderful if people were always acting to make sure that everyone was respected and valued. We know this is not how the world is working at this time. While a strict interpretation of this card might limit it to the courtroom, we can take a wider view to where the world needs more justice in any sense of the word.

Day 3 - Working the Title

Justice can be seen in many ways, depending on where we are looking. Fairness, justice, equality, or rightness might all be embodiments of this card.

1. What do you think about punishment?
2. Is rehabilitation possible?
3. Is forgiveness relevant to justice?
4. Is the letter of the law or its spirit more important?
5. Should religion and law mingle?

Look back over what you just wrote and note any words that stand out. Explore what other words you might use for this card. Grab a thesaurus if you want and explore other words that might cover the spectrum of ideas in this card more clearly for you. Of course, you can keep the traditional title if you like, too.

Day 4 - Exploring Further

The three elements we have been talking about all work together to create this card. Justice sits with equanimity between the polarities found in the tools they hold.

> Justice's "Three Elements" are:
>
> What represents balance?
> What is in their right hand?
> Where is the figure?

1. How do you find this equanimity in yourself?
2. What brings you back to centre?
3. How do you know when to judge?
4. How do you know when to forgive?
5. How do you know when you are "right"?
6. What injustice gets you the most worked up?
7. Around what parts of your life might justice find you wanting?
8. What evokes mercy in you?
9. What brings out severity in you?
10. How do you find the balance between these extremes?

When answering each of the questions for today, try to frame them in relationship to the three elements of Justice from Day 1.

Day 5 - Embodiment

Do the following. Do not worry. No one can see you, so just go for it!

Set a timer for eight minutes. Start chanting,

"I see the truth. I know what is right. I speak what is just."

Just let it all fall into jumbles. If your tongue slips, then repeat the slip. If you make sounds, repeat them. Allow it to flow into blabbering.

When the timer sounds, make a note of whatever came up. See if anything needs to be added to your card from this exploration.

Without thinking, write down the gesture Justice appeared to be making.

If you need to gather more images, do so once you are done writing.

Day 6 - Looking at Elements

Review your images, words, and notes from this week's work. For each of the three elements, choose what you like most and least and explore how to include both in the card.

With Justice, I have often struggled to find the balance – either being too forgiving or too harsh. The idea of equanimity is very important to my process. By endeavouring not to act immediately, I slow down the process so that my impulses become controlled. The metaphor that speaks strongly to me about this comes from karate, where, when bowing in, you make a fist with one hand and cover it with the other. The ability to fight is there, but it is held in check by peace – severity is bowing to mercy. It shows respect to all involved, and the context of a martial arts gym demonstrates that the rules are known. So I might show a person judging a competition, where two people are bowing in and making the gesture described, while the judge watches.

Day 7 - Combining the Elements

Put it all together. Hopefully, you have a good idea of what is in and out of the card now. Remember that including the three elements in your card in some way will help solidify its meaning. Justice's three elements are: *What represents balance? What is in their right hand? Where is the figure?* This is the day to create your card.

The Hermit

Day 1 - Opening to Imagery

Draw a card and invoke your synchronicity. (Refer to the instructions in the "Synchronistic Whatchamacallit" section of the Introduction). Write down the card you drew.

Roll your die once for each of the lists below. (The number will tell you which of the options to include on your card.)

What is the Hermit holding in their right hand?
1. A lamp
2. A flashlight
3. A crystal
4. The Sun
5. A flame
6. Nothing

What is the Hermit wearing?
1. Tattered robes
2. A monk's attire
3. A cloak
4. The starry sky
5. Jeans and a t-shirt
6. Animal furs

What are they doing?
1. Searching for something
2. Showing the way
3. Looking for dinner
4. Contemplating the mysteries
5. Waiting for their lover
6. Going home

As you work through this card, anytime you read "three elements" on another day's work, think back to these three questions and what the die chose for them.

Other elements you might consider including:

Are there animals on this card? What is going on in the background? Are they old or young?

Find, sketch, or write out as many possibilities for each as you can. Make sure to leave enough time to do this for all three ideas.

Day 2 – Putting It in Perspective

Before reading today's work (below), please take a moment to write down any synchronous message(s) or cue(s) you have received as a result of the card you drew yesterday.

*****

The Hermit is often taken as a wise person lighting the way for the world. They may variously represent the idea of withdrawal from the world, spiritual knowledge, or seeking wisdom, depending on the context. It is very important to understand what is motivating your Hermit. If they are wise, they will act differently than if they are seeking wisdom.

The Hermit is most often shown holding aloft a lantern. We can see this lamp as a tool of guidance – it lights the way for someone. The more esoterically inclined would go deeper and ask what is the light and where does it come from? It may be the light of spirit or perhaps the light of the Hermit, themselves. In making your card, the nature of this symbol will say a lot about the Hermit's nature. Are they modern or ancient, rooted in the world or more otherworldly, and so on.

The cloak of the Hermit conceals their mystery. Perhaps they have royal garb on under its enveloping folds. Maybe they are wearing such a humble garb out of necessity. The robe might be a sign of some religious vow they have sworn. I like to think of this robe as being a veil that hides something profound and inexplicable.

Where the Hermit is heading tells us about who they are, where they have been, and what their role in the world is. A wild Hermit living in a cave in the woods far from the world is very different from a monk living in a monastery. A pilgrim returning from their journey tells a very different story than if the pilgrim is just starting their journey.

Day 3 - Working the Title

The Hermit might be guide, guru, teacher, or madman. In all permutations, they represent truth and a way to find it.

1. Where does the truth live?
2. Do we need to socialize to thrive?
3. What is valuable about silence?
4. Is introversion/extroversion relevant to this card?
5. Can we learn everything on our own?

Look back over what you just wrote and note any words that stand out. Explore what other words you might use for this card. Grab a thesaurus if you want and explore other words that might cover the spectrum of ideas in this card more clearly for you. Of course, you can keep the traditional title if you like, too.

Day 4 - Exploring Further

The three elements we have been talking about all work together to create this card. The Hermit represents the way to navigate in the world (the lamp), a method of showing the truth they seek or serve (their attire), and where they are going (their destination).

> The Hermit's "Three Elements" are:
> What is in their right hand?
> What are they wearing?
> What are they doing?

1. What is your compass in life?
2. What shows the world your wisdom?
3. How will you know that you have arrived at your destination?
4. How do you choose your guides?
5. How do you choose your students?
6. In what ways have you learned from teachers?
7. How do you function as a guide in your world?
8. How do you handle isolation?
9. Do you fit in with the society in which you find yourself?
10. How would you feel meeting the Hermit on a dark road?

When answering each of the questions for today, try to frame them in relationship to the three elements of the Hermit from Day 1.

Day 5 - Embodiment

Do the following. Do not worry. No one can see you, so just go for it!

Set a timer for eight minutes. Start chanting,

> **"I light the way, in search of mysteries,
> as I wander the unknown."**

Just let it all fall into jumbles. If your tongue slips, then repeat the slip. If you make sounds, repeat them. Allow it to flow into blabbering.

When the timer sounds, make a note of whatever came up. See if anything needs to be added to your card from this exploration.

Without thinking, write down the gesture the Hermit appeared to be making.

If you need to gather more images, do so once you are done writing.

Day 6 - Looking at Elements

Review your images, words, and notes from this week's work. For each of the three elements, choose what you like most and least and explore how to include both in the card.

I rolled that the Hermit is holding a crystal, dressed in monk's robes, and going home. Though this card is about seeking wisdom, it can also be about guiding people. My wandering for truth is coming to an end. My Hermit might be more like the wise man that lives on the edge of town, to whom people travel to seek help. The days of going on retreat by myself for weeks at a time are behind me. Now, it is more about being in the world, while also being in touch with the other side.

Day 7 - Combining the Elements

Put it all together. Hopefully, you have a good idea of what is in and out of the card now. Remember that including the three elements in your card in some way will help solidify its meaning. The Hermit's three elements are: *What is in their right hand? What are they wearing? What are they doing?* This is the day to create your card.

The Wheel of Fortune

Day 1 - Opening to Imagery

Draw a card and invoke your synchronicity. (Refer to the instructions in the "Synchronistic Whatchamacallit" section of the Introduction). Write down the card you drew.

Roll your die once for each of the lists below. (The number will tell you which of the options to include on your card.)

Who is on the Wheel?
1. The traditional trio – a sphinx, a monkey, a crocodile
2. A man, a woman, and a child
3. The Alchemical elements – sulphur, salt, and mercury
4. Three gems
5. You: as a child, grown, and elderly
6. Three characters from the Majors

What is moving the Wheel?
1. Karma
2. Gravity
3. Spirit
4. Ego
5. Attachment
6. Desire

What is the Wheel made out of?
1. A Ferris wheel
2. A bicycle wheel
3. A baby carriage wheel
4. A water wheel
5. A hand-crank egg beater
6. A snake eating its own tail

As you work through this card, anytime you read "three elements" on another day's work, think back to these three questions and what the die chose for them.

Other elements you might consider including:

What is in the background? What is the centre of the Wheel? How many spokes in the Wheel? Is there a crank or machine making it move?

Find, sketch, or write out as many ideas for each as you can. Make sure to leave enough time to do this for all three ideas.

Day 2 - Putting It in Perspective

Before reading today's work (below), please take a moment to write down any synchronous message(s) or cue(s) you have received as a result of the card you drew yesterday.

*****

The Wheel of Fortune represents change and perhaps cause and effect, as well. We can add many other levels to what the Wheel is about, depending on the culture and tradition we layer on top of it. These cultural and religious layers also tell us how we should relate to the Wheel. Do we want off? To stay on top? Is it real? Or an illusion? Is there room for choice in relationship to it?

The characters on the Wheel often speak of a process: thesis, antithesis, and synthesis. An idea or action is set in motion. It encounters its opposite and is in some way challenged and broken down. The pieces are then recombined or added to in order to create a hybrid that is truer. We can also perceive it as the dance of how action, reaction, and consequences shape future actions.

"Change" could be a name for this card. Change is always brought about by something. It is the effect of some force, action, or decision. If we believe the force that moves the Wheel is controllable, it creates a very different card than if we think it is a cosmic law beyond our control. I was amazed at how much the idea of karma disempowered a lot of the people I met in India. Perhaps it is wisdom to accept the movement of the universe. My western mind struggles to accept it.

The construction of the Wheel is certainly not accidental. The manner in which it is made allows the Wheel to fulfill its function, but it also tells us more about why it is there and what it implies for us as we try to deal with it. If our imagery references childhood, that we can read as accumulation of experience. Other constructions, like the Ferris wheel, imply that we can get on and off the Wheel.

Day 3 - Working the Title

The Wheel explores ideas of control, fate, destiny, choice, and freedom. Our lives play out at the intersection of these possibilities and forces.

1. How does free will factor into living?
2. How much can we control life?
3. Is there a guiding force behind life?
4. Do past lives impact this one?
5. Are there lessons we must learn?

Look back over what you just wrote and note any words that stand out. Explore what other words you might use for this card. Grab a thesaurus if you want and explore other words that might cover the spectrum of ideas in this card more clearly for you. Of course, you can keep the traditional title if you like, too.

Day 4 - Exploring Further

The three elements we have been talking about all work together to create this card. The Wheel of Fortune combines the three elements we rolled for on the first day to fulfill its function. The characters on the Wheel act and react in relationship to the force that moves the Wheel. The construction of the Wheel defines the experience and its limits. It may also add more levels of intention to the function of the Wheel.

> Fortune's "Three Elements" are:
> Who is on the Wheel?
> What is moving the Wheel?
> What is the Wheel made of?

1. How do the three characters on the Wheel relate to each other?
2. What beliefs are implied by the Wheel?
3. How is control or lack of control in life expressed in this card?
4. Which characters do you want to be in this card?
5. What would your ideal way of relating to this card be?
6. Do you believe in fate?
7. How easily do you embrace change?

When answering each of the questions for today, try to frame them in relationship to the three elements of the Wheel of Fortune from Day 1.

Day 5 - Embodiment

Do the following. Do not worry. No one can see you, so just go for it!

Set a timer for eight minutes. Start chanting,

"The Wheel will turn: up is now down, until it is up again."

Just let it all fall into jumbles. If your tongue slips, then repeat the slip. If you make sounds, repeat them. Allow it to flow into blabbering.

When the timer sounds, make a note of whatever came up. See if anything needs to be added to your card from this exploration.

If you need to gather more images, do so once you are done writing.

Day 6 - Looking at Elements

Review your images, words, and notes from this week's work. For each of the three elements, choose what you like most and least and explore how to include both in the card.

I am, in my heart, tied to the idea of karma and non-attachment. I work to be the unmoving centre of the Wheel. That is freedom and power. Of course, many forces encourage me to move back to the outside of the Wheel at times too. I like the idea of a Ferris wheel, with twelve cars for the wheel of the zodiac around the outside. I also like the traditional three characters representing thesis, antithesis, and synthesis. They may all ride in the same car, or separately. Collectively, it shows the change that is possible and recognizes we can get off the ride at any time.

Day 7 - Combining the Elements

Put it all together. Hopefully, you have a good idea of what is in and out of the card now. Remember that including the three elements in your card in some way will help solidify its meaning. The Wheel of Fortune's three elements are: *Who is on the wheel? What is moving the wheel? What is the wheel made of?* This is the day to create your card.

Strength

Day 1 - Opening to Imagery

Draw a card and invoke your synchronicity. (Refer to the instructions in the "Synchronistic Whatchamacallit" section of the Introduction). Write down the card you drew.

Roll your die once for each of the lists below. (The number will tell you which of the options to include on your card.)

What beast is shown in this card?
1. A lion
2. A dragon
3. A devil
4. A human
5. A shadow
6. A wolf

How is the person dressed?
1. In a robe
2. As a warrior
3. As a priest
4. Cargo shorts and a t-shirt
5. In your favourite outfit
6. With fig leaves

How do the two characters relate to each other?
1. The person calmly controls the beast
2. They are both calm
3. They are wrestling
4. They are avoiding each other
5. The beast has the upper hand
6. They are unaware of each other

As you work through this card, anytime you read "three elements" on another day's work, think back to these three questions and what the die chose for them.

Other elements you might consider including:

Are there other forces at play in this card? What, or who is watching this scene? Where is it playing out?

Find, sketch, or write out as many possibilities for each as you can. Make sure to leave enough time to do this for all three ideas.

Day 2 - Putting It in Perspective

Before reading today's work (below), please take a moment to write down any synchronous message(s) or cue(s) you have received as a result of the card you drew yesterday.

*****

The Strength card represents the ideals of purity, control and focus. It is said that the card shows a virgin taming the beast with her purity. This may be so, yet the strength this card speaks of is rarely about what is going on in the world. It represents the conquering of the inner duality and conflicts that we often struggle with. Purity here can be religious, moral, or singularity of focus.

What beasts seek to consume us? The lion represents both wildness and courage. It contains both what we seek and what we fear. Our fears are often a complicated mix of reality and projection. How likely is a lion to eat us? If it is hungry, we are certainly on the menu. A well-fed circus lion might have much less interest in us. We could be at more risk from a desperate human than the king of the jungle.

The person pictured in this card speaks to the taming or controlling influence. Their attire shows what power they are using to deal with this beast. Their power may come from their religious convictions, strength of character, or ability to just be who they are.

Traditions vary the ways in which the lion and the person relate to each other. Most commonly, the person holds the lion's mouth open. However, we also see them elsewhere standing calmly together. In Crowley's Lust card, we see a woman riding the lion. The relationship between the two reveals to us deeper secrets and possibilities. It can be instructive in a reading, "Ride the beast," or revealing, "You seem afraid of your strength."

Day 3 - Working the Title

The Strength card shows us ways of controlling both ourselves and the world. It also speaks to our relationship to power and focus.

1. How do you relate to power?
2. Do you feel people should control themselves?
3. When might wildness need to be free of control?
4. What does the beast want from the person?
5. What does the person want from the beast?
6. What lessons are implied by the two characters' relationship?

Look back over what you just wrote and note any words that stand out. Explore what other words you might use for this card. Grab a thesaurus if you want and explore other words that might cover the spectrum of ideas in this card more clearly for you. Of course, you can keep the traditional title if you like, too.

Day 4 - Exploring Further

The three elements we have been talking about all work together to create this card. Strength is the interplay between two opposite forces, the person and the beast, and the way in which they interact. The image of the beast reveals its nature, as does the attire of the figure. In their relating to each other, we can see how strength may be found or lost.

> Strength's "Three Elements" are:
>
> What beast is shown?
> How is the person dressed?
> How do the two relate to each other?

1. Do you prefer one character on the card over the other?
2. What do you wish they were doing instead?
3. What fears have you learned to control?
4. How do you know if you can trust an animal?
5. What might give you more strength?

When answering each of the questions for today, try to frame them in relationship to the three elements of Strength from Day 1.

Day 5 - Embodiment

Do the following. Do not worry. No one can see you, so just go for it!

Set a timer for eight minutes. Start chanting,

"In peace or power, hear me roar, for I am mighty."

Just let it all fall into jumbles. If your tongue slips, then repeat the slip. If you make sounds, repeat them. Allow it to flow into blabbering.

When the timer sounds, make a note of whatever came up. See if anything needs to be added to your card from this exploration.

Without thinking, write down the gesture the person appeared to be making.

If you need to gather more images, do so once you are done writing.

Day 6 - Looking at Elements

Review your images, words, and notes from this week's work. For each of the three elements, choose what you like most and least and explore how to include both in the card.

In rolling for myself, I got a devil, dressed in fig leaves, and wrestling. A very biblical combination of imagery. Yet I am not fond of seeing this card in a moralistic way. Perhaps I spent too many years studying Crowley to be really judgemental of my humanity. I am fond of the notion of purity – or perhaps better put, authenticity – as the road to strength. In my life, the avoidance or denial of parts of myself leads to the appearance of devils. When I am in tune with my whole self, everything is in balance or control. Denying the shadowy sides, however, undermines the other sides of my world. So, in the end,

I would have the two wrestling, but enjoying the dance. Showering off of them would be creativity and joy. A playful combat, instead of a serious one.

Day 7 - Combining the Elements

Put it all together. Hopefully, you have a good idea of what is in and out of the card now. Remember that including the three elements in your card in some way will help solidify its meaning. Strength's three elements are: *What beast is shown? How is the person dressed? How do the two relate to each other?* This is the day to create your card.

The Hanged Man

Day 1 - Opening to Imagery

Draw a card and invoke your synchronicity. (Refer to the instructions in the "Synchronistic Whatchamacallit" section of the Introduction). Write down the card you drew.

Roll your die once for each of the lists below. (The number will tell you which of the options to include on your card.)

What is the Hanged Man strung up by?
1. A rope
2. A snake
3. An electronics cable
4. An ankh
5. A vine
6. A clothes peg

How do they look?
1. Sad
2. Hurt
3. Desperate
4. Angry
5. Playful
6. Defiant

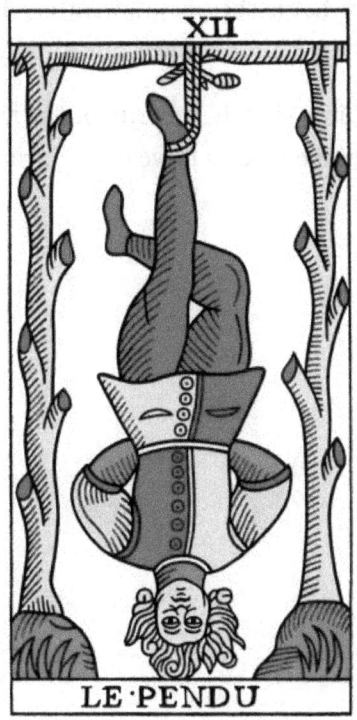

Who is there with them?
1. No one
2. An executioner
3. A midwife
4. The Hierophant
5. The police
6. A crowd

As you work through this card, anytime you read "three elements" on another day's work, think back to these three questions and what the die chose for them.

Other elements you might consider including:

What is the person wearing? In what position is their body? Are they fully bound, or just hung up by a body part?

Find, sketch, or write out as many possibilities for each as you can. Make sure to leave enough time to do this for all three ideas.

Day 2 - Putting It in Perspective

Before reading today's work (below), please take a moment to write down any synchronous message(s) or cue(s) you have received as a result of the card you drew yesterday.

*****

The Hanged Man represents being stuck. We could be stuck for any number of reasons. It might be a punishment, or we might just be gestating. In some ways, we can see this card as a child waiting to make their way out of the womb and into the world, or somewhere on their journey.

The mechanism suspending this person informs us about what forces put them there. If they are hung by their iPhone charger, it speaks of certain ideas, while a hangman's noose speaks of a very different set of ideas. If we include what they are hanging from, the manner of being hung up allows us to infer many things about the system that put them there, too. Is it constructed just for this purpose? Or was it a convenient item? A schoolyard football goal post reveals something quite different than a gallows.

If we look at the face of the Hanged Man, we can see something about their nature. In the *Noblet Tarot de Marseille*, the person is sticking out their tongue, as if to mock those who have put them there. This card can be linked to the idea of the crucifixion, too. Christ on the cross might be shown in agony or grace, depending on how the artist felt about the crucifixion. Rebellious or compliant? Pained or transformed? These polarities tell us a lot about the story of how they got here.

Most decks show the Hanged Man without anyone else around. Yet, historically, this card would have likely been a public spectacle. Crowds might have thrown rotten fruit at a scoundrel, or perhaps the guards would hold back an outraged crowd. This card, while it is often interpreted as an inner experience, is certainly public in its implications. The events that follow the moment shown in this card – a cart carrying the body to a grave or a return to life – take the energy of this card further into the world.

Day 3 - Working the Title

The Hanged Man can represent withdrawal, a yogi's meditation, a period of gestation, an initiation, a punishment, or an execution.

1. What is your relationship to the idea of punishment?
2. How do you relate to asceticism?
3. Is stuckness part of the natural cycle of life?
4. What value does sacrifice have?
5. What can be learned from being trapped?

Look back over what you just wrote and note any words that stand out. Explore what other words you might use for this card. Grab a thesaurus if you want and explore other words that might cover the spectrum of ideas in this card more clearly for you. Of course, you can keep the traditional title if you like, too.

Day 4 - Exploring Further

The three elements we have been talking about all work together to create this card. The Hanged Man is suspended in some manner. They react to being there in some way. Someone is there to support their original reason for being there.

> The Hanged Man's "Three Elements" are:
>
> What are they hung up by?
> What is their expression?
> Who is with them, if anyone?

1. What binds you?
2. How do you hold yourself accountable?
3. How do you know when it is time to let go and move on?
4. Who do you wish was with you?
5. How do you know if you deserve your situation?
6. What might be stuck in your life right now?
7. How could time gestating serve you?
8. What help might you need in transformations that take time?
9. In what ways are you punishing yourself?

When answering each of the questions for today, try to frame them in relationship to the three elements of the Hanged Man from Day 1.

Day 5 - Embodiment

Do the following. Do not worry. No one can see you, so just go for it!

Set a timer for eight minutes. Start chanting,

"I hang, I dangle, I swing, I sway, and I wait."

Just let it all fall into jumbles. If your tongue slips, then repeat the slip. If you make sounds, repeat them. Allow it to flow into blabbering.

When the timer sounds, make a note of whatever came up. See if anything needs to be added to your card from this exploration.

Without thinking, write down the gesture the Hanged Man appeared to be making.

If you need to gather more images, do so once you are done writing.

Day 6 - Looking at Elements

Review your images, words, and notes from this week's work. For each of the three elements, choose what you like most and least and explore how to include both in the card.

I am a very motivated Sagittarius. I don't usually enjoy waiting, so this card can be a frustrating one for me. I rolled and got clothes peg, looking sad, and the police. The clothes peg reminds me of childhood and points towards the ways in which I felt sad when at home. The police remind me of forces that cannot be reasoned with. Especially, at the time of writing this, with all the cases of unarmed people of colour people being killed in the USA. Together, they point out a danger that is going on or breaking beyond what is safe. Yet I am not a child, so in my case, I'd reverse the people and have the police dangling off of a clothesline, while a child dances freely.

Day 7 - Combining the Elements

Put it all together. Hopefully, you have a good idea of what is in and out of the card now. Remember that including the three elements in your card in some way will help solidify its meaning. The Hanged Man's three elements are: *What they are hung up by? What is their facial expression? Who is with them if anyone?* This is the day to create your card.

Death

Day 1 - Opening to Imagery

Draw a card and invoke your synchronicity. (Refer to the instructions in the "Synchronistic Whatchamacallit" section of the Introduction). Write down the card you drew.

Roll your die once for each of the lists below. (The number will tell you which of the options to include on your card.)

How does Death show up in this card?
1. As a skeleton
2. As Chronos
3. As a worm
4. As a clock
5. As an open grave
6. As a child

What is Death wielding?
1. A scythe
2. A machete
3. A paper shredder
4. An hourglass
5. A key
6. Nothing

13 ~ Death

Death from the beautiful *Gaian Tarot* by Joanna Powell Colbert is a wonderful example of a break from what we are used to seeing that still respects the traditional meanings.

Who or what else do we see in the card?
1. You
2. Fields of crops
3. Body parts
4. The character from another card
5. A child
6. An elderly person

As you work through this card, anytime you read "three elements" on another day's work, think back to these three questions and what the die chose for them.

Other elements you might consider including:

Are there any emblems on Death's clothing? Are there features in the background outside of Death's attention? How is Death standing?

Find, sketch, or write out as many possibilities for each as you can. Make sure to leave enough time to do this for all three ideas.

Day 2 - Putting It in Perspective

Before reading today's work (below), please take a moment to write down any synchronous message(s) or cue(s) you have received as a result of the card you drew yesterday.

*****

Death represents change, endings, and transformations. Trump XIII is also one of the most feared cards in the deck. We can try to interpret it positively, but we all know on some level that we will meet this character someday. We all hope it will be a long time in the future, but at the same time part of us knows Death's arrival is beyond our knowing.

Death's appearance tells us the nature of death in our life. It can reveal to us our relationship to death and the ideas of change. Are we accepting of transformation or does it intimidate us. Is it natural or gross? How we feel about our bodies might even get tied into how Death appears to us. It can be gruesome, fearsome, comforting, welcome, or joyous.

Death's tool conveys even more information about what is going on in this card. The tool here shows us both the approach and the pace. Does Death arrive a little at a time? Perhaps even with time to avoid running into it? Or is it a sudden force that explodes into our life, carrying us off into what is next? Perhaps it sneaks up in the shadows, waiting to see if we have the courage to look into the growing darkness and see what is there.

The items or people being acted on in the card provide us with another layer of meaning. Is it close to us or abstracted? In some decks, we see no bodies at all, and in others we see kings and queens. In our modern life it is very foreign to spend any amount of time with a corpse. In other cultures and times, we might have had a much more immediate relationship with the corpse of a loved one.

Day 3 - Working the Title

Death shows us what must end. It guides us towards how we should handle these endings for ourselves and others. Death allows life to thrive.

1. What do you think happens after death?
2. Can we control the end of our lives?
3. Do you think we will live forever someday?
4. What would happen without people dying?
5. Are there moral issues around people choosing to die?

Look back over what you just wrote and note any words that stand out. Explore what other words you might use for this card. Grab a thesaurus if you want and explore other words that might cover the spectrum of ideas in this card more clearly for you. Of course, you can keep the traditional title if you like, too.

Day 4 - Exploring Further

The three elements we have been talking about all work together to create this card. Death swings its scythe at a person, and they die. The way your three elements combine to show death in action will reveal deeper mysteries.

> Death's "Three Elements" are:
>
> How is Death shown?
> What are they wielding?
> What else is in the card?

1. How would you like to go?
2. Are you afraid of death?
3. How do you grieve?
4. How might you welcome the change this card brings?
5. How much intervention would you want in order to avoid meeting your end?
6. How do you feel about euthanasia?
7. How do you know when it is time to end something?
8. When should you check your friendships or relationships to see if they still have a pulse?

When answering each of the questions for today, try to frame them in relationship to the three elements of Death from Day 1.

Day 5 - Embodiment

Do the following. Do not worry. No one can see you, so just go for it!

Set a timer for eight minutes. Start chanting,

"What was is gone. What was is done. I carry on."

Just let it all fall into jumbles. If your tongue slips, then repeat the slip. If you make sounds, repeat them. Allow it to flow into blabbering.

When the timer sounds, make a note of whatever came up. See if anything needs to be added to your card from this exploration.

Without thinking, write down the gesture Death appeared to be making.

If you need to gather more images, do so once you are done writing.

Day 6 - Looking at Elements

Review your images, words, and notes from this week's work. For each of the three elements, choose what you like most and least and explore how to include both in the card.

I spent time in India, where I got to see the people there and their very different relationship to death. In Varanasi, they bring the bodies to edge of the Ganges and cremate them. They have been washed by the family and wrapped in cloth. The body is put on a pyre and lit from a fire that has been burning for 5000 years. Ceremonies are performed and tears shed. It takes about three hours for the body to be turned to ash. Whatever remains is swept into the river. Some kinds of sacred people are thought to not need to be purified. Children, pregnant women, and holy men are instead submerged with a large rock in the middle of the river. Of course, often parts of them resurface. One hundred feet downstream, families are bathing, doing their laundry, and brushing their teeth – all in the river. Life flows constantly with death. This is what my Death card would show.

Day 7 - Combining the Elements

Put it all together. Hopefully, you have a good idea of what is in and out of the card now. Remember that including the three elements in your card in some way will help solidify its meaning. Death's three elements are: *How is Death shown? What are they wielding? What else is in the card?* This is the day to create your card.

Temperance

Day 1 - Opening to Imagery

Draw a card and invoke your synchronicity. (Refer to the instructions in the "Synchronistic Whatchamacallit" section of the Introduction). Write down the card you drew.

Roll your die once for each of the lists below. (The number will tell you which of the options to include on your card.)

What kind of figure shows up in this card?
1. An angel
2. A man
3. A woman
4. A sphinx
5. Pure light
6. A hermaphrodite

What is in their right hand?
1. Fire
2. A wand
3. A sword
4. A crystal
5. A gesture you decide
6. A closed fist

What is in their left hand?
1. A cup
2. A coin
3. Water
4. A crystal
5. A gesture you decide
6. An open hand

As you work through this card, anytime you read "three elements" on another day's work, think back to these three questions and what the die chose for them.

Other elements you might consider including:

Is anyone else there? Are they in a holy place or a common one? Are the items, or hands interacting with each other?

Find, sketch, or write out as many possibilities for each as you can. Make sure to leave enough time to do this for all three ideas.

Day 2 - Putting It in Perspective

Before reading today's work (below), please take a moment to write down any synchronous message(s) or cue(s) you have received as a result of the card you drew yesterday.

*****

Though Temperance is usually framed as the union of two opposite things, it really is the merging of three things. The fire and water, or water going between vessels, is bound together through the action of spirit. All three come together to create something new. This card is one of balance, harmony, unity, and transcendence.

Usually this card shows an angel as the central figure. Obviously, this is the spirit aspect of the card. This character is the one who is acting on everything else at play in the card. This figure is the alchemist in the lab transforming lead into gold. They are the wisdom in the self bringing out the best in the person. In many ways this figure represents the aspiration or hope that the querant this card speaks to is working towards.

The right side of the body, and certainly the right hand, are seen as active. This is why we often see fire in this hand. Whatever is found in this hand is having an influence, going out into the world, or impacting the situation. Often it is about expansion and movement. When we consider the title – Temperance – we can say that what is in the right hand is what needs tempering.

The left hand is most often seen as being the passive or receptive hand. It is the one that receives from the world, instead of transmitting. It is often about contracting, channeling, or containing. When we consider the title – Temperance – we can say that what is in the left hand is what does the tempering.

Day 3 - Working the Title

Temperance is a card that allows us to find balance, harmony, and certainty about our path in life. It keeps us from going off the road and into the ditch of life.

1. How do you feel about moderation?
2. Is this card about balance or flow?
3. Is this a higher power, or a part of the self?
4. Is temperance a moral or practical idea for you?
5. How does the idea of uniting relate to this card?

Look back over what you just wrote and note any words that stand out. Explore what other words you might use for this card. Grab a thesaurus if you want and explore other words that might cover the spectrum of ideas in this card more clearly for you. Of course, you can keep the traditional title if you like, too.

Day 4 - Exploring Further

The three elements we have been talking about all work together to create this card. Temperance is the figure using two extremes, one in each hand, to bring harmony as a whole.

> Temperance's "Three Elements" are:
> What kind of figure is shown?
> What is in their right hand?
> What is in their left hand?

1. What in your life tempers you?
2. Are the extremes necessary?
3. Where does the wisdom to find the balance come from?
4. Is it possible to live in this energy all the time?
5. When might it be wise to let one hand direct things more?
6. Are we judged by the average of our actions, or by how close we live to the centre?
7. What brings you back into alignment?
8. What do you aspire to spiritually?
9. What needs tempering in your life?

When answering each of the questions for today, try to frame them in relationship to the three elements of Temperance from Day 1.

Day 5 - Embodiment

Do the following. Do not worry. No one can see you, so just go for it!

Set a timer for eight minutes. Start chanting,

"Hot or cold, hard or soft, bring balance to my soul."

Just let it all fall into jumbles. If your tongue slips, then repeat the slip. If you make sounds, repeat them. Allow it to flow into blabbering.

When the timer sounds, make a note of whatever came up. See if anything needs to be added to your card from this exploration.

Without thinking, write down the gesture Temperance appeared to be making.

If you need to gather more images, do so once you are done writing.

Day 6 - Looking at Elements

Review your images, words, and notes from this week's work. For each of the three elements, choose what you like most and least and explore how to include both in the card.

For me, this card is always tied to the ideas of aspiration and transformation. As a human, I aspire to unite with the divine. To achieve this, the opposites of my life must be brought into unity or harmony. The fuel for this rocket journey into the outer realms of human experience comes from the combustion of the opposites. My card would have an angel at the top and a rocket ship with two "jets," one of water and the other of fire, sending it off into space.

Day 7 - Combining the Elements

Put it all together. Hopefully, you have a good idea of what is in and out of the card now. Remember that including the three elements in your card in some way will help solidify its meaning. Temperance's three elements are: *What kind of figure is shown? What is in their right hand? What is in their left hand?* This is the day to create your card.

The Devil

Day 1 - Opening to Imagery

Draw a card and invoke your synchronicity. (Refer to the instructions in the "Synchronistic Whatchamacallit" section of the Introduction). Write down the card you drew.

Roll your die once for each of the lists below. (The number will tell you which of the options to include on your card.)

What kind of devil shows up in this card?
1. Baphomet
2. An abomination
3. A slick, suit-wearing devil
4. A goat
5. A seductive devil
6. It is obscured

What do the two figures look like?
1. Normal humans
2. Imps
3. Adam and Eve
4. Children
5. Symbols
6. There are many people, not just two

How are the figures contained?
1. By chains
2. In boxes
3. They are not
4. By roots
5. A locked door
6. By magick

As you work through this card, anytime you read "three elements" on another day's work, think back to these three questions and what the die chose for them.

Other elements you might consider:

Are there other beings present? What is the scenery like? What is the Devil sitting on?

Find, sketch, or write out as many possibilities for each as you can. Make sure to leave enough time to do this for all three ideas.

Day 2 - Putting It in Perspective

Before reading today's work (below), please take a moment to write down any synchronous message(s) or cue(s) you have received as a result of the card you drew yesterday.

*****

The Devil card is about the interaction of the protagonist, the Devil, with the other characters in the scene. Every player in this card has an agenda that has brought them to be in the situation we see. We often assume that there is a negative scene being played out, but perhaps they agreed to this. Perhaps it is the Devil who is bound and the rest are controlling him.

When we are talking about the Devil, his manner of being represented will tell us a lot about his motivations. If we see a Titan like Chronos, we know that it is about primal untamed power and the destructive aspects of the unknown. If instead we see Prometheus, we can interpret this diabolical fellow as a liberator of humanity. A serpent might lead us to a more biblical temptress idea instead.

The two figures are usually some depiction of a man and women. Their nature defines their relationship to the Devil. If we see Adam and Eve, we can infer that they have been tempted out of the garden and are paying for their disobedience. If instead we see a more bacchanal scene going on, the satyrs and maenads might be just revellers in a procession. Who these characters are determines their attitudes towards the Devil.

The restraint, or its absence, in this card is the final part of the equation. A satyr might be willingly going along with the Devil, but if he is chained, we can infer a subconscious restraint. The visible chain mirrors a hidden, unconscious one. If they are all in a locked room together, perhaps they are more complicit in their circumstance.

Day 3 - Working the Title

The Devil represents pleasure, sensuality, material gain, addiction, and enslavement. The Devil makes life worth living, or a living hell, depending on our actions.

1. Is the Devil necessary?
2. What would be a good use for the Devil?
3. Can this card be life affirming?
4. How do you know this card when you see it in a person or in the world?
5. Are these elements in harmony?
6. Is there a conflict between spirit and the material world?
7. Is this an inevitable part of human nature?
8. What wisdom is in this card?

Look back over what you just wrote and note any words that stand out. Explore what other words you might use for this card. Grab a thesaurus if you want and explore other words that might cover the spectrum of ideas in this card more clearly for you. Of course, you can keep the traditional title if you like, too.

Day 4 - Exploring Further

The three elements we have been talking about all work together to create this card. The Devil is the beast in the middle, the two figures, and the thing that contains them.

> The Devil's
> "Three Elements" are:
>
> What kind of devil is shown?
> How do the two figures look?
> How are the figures contained?

1. What appeals to you about the Devil?
2. How would you feel about people who choose to spend time with him?
3. What fun would you want to have if you knew there were no consequences?
4. In what situations would you give up your power?
5. For what would you make a deal with the Devil? ("Nothing" isn't a valid answer to this one.)
6. Who represents this card in your life?

When answering each of the questions for today, try to frame them in relationship to the three elements of the Devil from Day 1.

Day 5 - Embodiment

Do the following. Do not worry. No one can see you, so just go for it!

Set a timer for eight minutes. Start chanting,

"Shadow of the world. Spirit on Earth. Singer of songs."

Just let it all fall into jumbles. If your tongue slips, then repeat the slip. If you make sounds, repeat them. Allow it to flow into blabbering.

When the timer sounds, make a note of whatever came up. See if anything needs to be added to your card from this exploration.

Without thinking, write down the gesture the Devil appeared to be making.

If you need to gather more images, do so once you are done writing.

Day 6 - Looking at Elements

Review your images, words, and notes from this week's work. For each of the three elements, choose what you like most and least and explore how to include both in the card.

The Devil, to me, is about understanding yourself. Not just the parts you like, but those shadowy and perhaps socially unacceptable parts that we all have and wish were not there. My Devil would be Bacchus and the people, masked revellers. No one would be bound, but vines from grapes would wind through everything, creating the possibility of becoming trapped. This card is one of everything in moderation, including moderation. Living here all the time is destructive. Visiting this card is a wonderful escape.

Day 7 - Combining the Elements

Put it all together. Hopefully, you have a good idea of what is in and out of the card now. Remember that including the three elements in your card in some way will help solidify its meaning. The Devil's three elements are: *What kind of devil is shown? How do the two figures look? How are the figures contained?* This is the day to create your card.

The Tower

Day 1 - Opening to Imagery

Draw a card and invoke your synchronicity. (Refer to the instructions in the "Synchronistic Whatchamacallit" section of the Introduction). Write down the card you drew.

Roll your die once for each of the lists below. (The number will tell you which of the options to include on your card.)

What kind of building is in the card?
1. A tower
2. A highrise
3. A suburban house
4. A hut
5. A cave
6. A church

What is striking the Tower?
1. Lightning
2. Fire
3. A spaceship
4. A spear
5. Explosives
6. An imaginary animal

Who, or what, is falling from the Tower?
1. Two people
2. A sun and moon
3. Money
4. Crystals
5. Daily items (furniture, etc.)
6. Old photographs

As you work through this card, anytime you read "three elements" on another day's work, think back to these three questions and what the die chose for them.

Other elements you might consider including:

Is there something sending the lightning or other force in the card? Are there people watching? How much of the Tower stays standing?

Find, sketch, or write out as many possibilities for each as you can. Make sure to leave enough time to do this for all three ideas.

Day 2 - Putting It in Perspective

Before reading today's work (below), please take a moment to write down any synchronous message(s) or cue(s) you have received as a result of the card you drew yesterday.

*****

The Tower is most often seen as a man-made structure with the top being struck by lightning, or fire. From this building, two people fall. The relationship between these elements tells us a lot about what is actually going on. Is it divine punishment? Was this a natural disaster? Further adding to the mix is the idea that this card was called the "House of God" in many older decks. In the dance between these ideas, we can say for sure that there is disruption or change happening. The elements and their interaction will tell us the rest.

The building itself informs us about the nature of the ambition or motivation that brought us to this card. Some say this card is the Tower of Babel, rising arrogantly to reach heaven. Perhaps it is a building of piousness seeking to glorify spirit instead? Towers are often depicted as being military in nature. Is this about war, or defence against some unseen protagonists? What kind of life did the builders of this building aspire to? If your roll of the die gave you a natural structure, why would people choose to live there?

The Tower is often shown being struck by lightning. We can choose to view this as either a natural event or, alternatively, as divine wrath. Or perhaps it is being pelted by the canons of some opposing army? In the nature of what is striking the Tower, we find reasons for the current situation. Of course, tied to this is the question of whether or not the Tower falls. Is it levelled by the forces working against it, or does it have the inner structural strength to stand?

When we see two people falling from the Tower, I often start to think about what duality is important. Are they a man and woman? Is it about class, age, wealth, the conscious, the unconscious? What divides, unites, or connects these two people or things. Finally, we need to consider their demeanour – are they afraid, or happy with the fall? Are they hurt by the fall, or are they okay?

Day 3 - Working the Title

The Tower speaks of swift change that is usually unexpected.

1. Is the idea of divine punishment relevant?
2. What is enduring in life?
3. How does a divine plan fit into this card?
4. How can we secure ourselves against chance?
5. How high is too high?
6. Where is the boundary between aspiration and arrogance?

Look back over what you just wrote and note any words that stand out. Explore what other words you might use for this card. Grab a thesaurus if you want and explore other words that might cover the spectrum of ideas in this card more clearly for you. Of course, you can keep the traditional title if you like, too.

Day 4 - Exploring Further

The three elements we have been talking about all work together to create this card. The Tower is the combination of a force reaching up, the building, a force reaching down, the lightning, and the consequences, the falling people.

> The Tower's "Three Elements" are:
>
> What kind of building is shown?
> What is striking the Tower?
> What is falling from the Tower?

1. When have you experienced big unexpected change?
2. How do you weather change?
3. Do you think we can stay in balance?
4. Who or what would you throw a lightning bolt at?
5. What in your life are you waiting to be punished for?
6. What are you afraid is going to fall apart or get knocked down?

When answering each of the questions for today, try to frame them in relationship to the three elements of the Tower from Day 1.

Day 5 - Embodiment

Do the following. Do not worry. No one can see you, so just go for it!

Set a timer for eight minutes. Start chanting,

> **"Strike and shake. Fire and quake.**
> **Time for it to come on down."**

Just let it all fall into jumbles. If your tongue slips, then repeat the slip. If you make sounds, repeat them. Allow it to flow into blabbering.

When the timer sounds, make a note of whatever came up. See if anything needs to be added to your card from this exploration.

Without thinking, write down anything around this card that must be added to fit your experience.

If you need to gather more images, do so once you are done writing.

Day 6 - Looking at Elements

Review your images, words, and notes from this week's work. For each of the three elements, choose what you like most and least and explore how to include both in the card.

My rolls for this card were a suburban house, being hit by a spaceship, with money pouring out. I grew up in suburbia, and to me it was always an alien thing. The idea of an "other" culture, the spaceship, implies a radically different point of view. Certainly, from my current point of view, it is questionable whether or not it is ecologically and socially a viable structure. The money pouring out of it speaks of the rebalancing of things on the one hand, and on the other hand, we have the idea of the cost associated with this decentralized car-culture structure we have created. Time will tell what kind of rebalancing will come. Though I feel like this writing might be read as a moralizing, I actually see the spaceship as a metaphor for awakening to a higher level of consciousness. What changes when we become global citizens? How about interstellar dwellers?

Day 7 - Combining the Elements

Put it all together. Hopefully, you have a good idea of what is in and out of the card now. Remember that including the three elements in your card in some way will help solidify its meaning. The Tower's three elements are: *What kind of building is shown? What is striking the Tower? What is falling from the Tower?* This is the day to create your card.

The Star

Day 1 - Opening to Imagery

Draw a card and invoke your synchronicity. (Refer to the instructions in the "Synchronistic Whatchamacallit" section of the Introduction). Write down the card you drew.

Roll your die once for each of the lists below. (The number will tell you which of the options to include on your card.)

What are the "stars"?
1. One star
2. Many stars
3. The planets
4. Crystals
5. A spiralling galaxy
6. Entities

Who is the figure in the card?
1. A naked woman
2. You
3. The Goddess
4. An astrologer
5. The night sky
6. Mother of the universe

What is being poured out of the pitchers?
(If you feel the two containers hold different things, roll twice.)
1. Water
2. Souls
3. Wisdom
4. Healing
5. Love
6. Hope

As you work through this card, anytime you read "three elements" on another day's work, think back to these three questions and what the die chose for them.

Other elements you might consider including:

What are the pitchers being poured into? Is anyone/anything else on the scene? Where is this happening?

Find, sketch, or write out as many possibilities for each as you can. Make sure to leave enough time to do this for all three ideas.

Day 2 - Putting It in Perspective

Before reading today's work (below), please take a moment to write down any synchronous message(s) or cue(s) you have received as a result of the card you drew yesterday.

*****

When looking at this card, it can be about many things depending on the perspective we are viewing it from. The Star, when looked at in sequence, is the return of the light after journeying through the challenges of the Devil and the Tower. On its own it can stand for guidance – navigating by the stars, and seeing the way forward. It can also speak of profound transcendence, suggesting that we have gone beyond ourselves and started to connect with the universe at an astronomical level.

When exploring what the stars are in this card, we are pushed to ponder about what structure or order is at play. The stars move in an orderly orbit and reveal the hidden forces at work in creation or in ourselves. Just as the movements of the planets and stars reveal gravity to an astronomer, the same movements reveal our nature to the astrologer. What we see in the heavens in this card shows us what the universe is and who we are.

The figure in this card represents an intermediary between the celestial energies in the sky and the world that they libate from containers they hold. Whom or what we find uniting these levels of creation influences and informs the nature of the connection. Usually, the woman on this card seems tranquil and benign. Yet the water here could flood the world and wash it clean if they are enacting the story of Noah and the ark. Who they are and why they are pouring water will tell us a lot about what is going on here.

Often it is said that the figure is renewing the world with her waters. Crowley says that one cup pours the infinite possibilities of creation into the world, and the other, the sweet ambrosia of creation that makes life worth living. Perhaps it is a cooling and healing balm after the harsh fiery energy of the Tower. If we see this "water" as the flowing of understanding from the celestial level to the material, it could also stand to represent the wisdom found in the journey through the Trumps.

Day 3 - Working the Title

The Star speaks of patterns, our nature, the big picture, destiny, fate, and the possibility of renewal.

1. Is there a grand plan at work in creation?
2. How can we know what that plan is?
3. How much control do we have over our lives?
4. What significance does having an intermediary, the figure, have for this card?
5. How is this connection different than the Hermit's connection to Source?

Look back over what you just wrote and note any words that stand out. Explore what other words you might use for this card. Grab a thesaurus if you want and explore other words that might cover the spectrum of ideas in this card more clearly for you. Of course, you can keep the traditional title if you like, too.

Day 4 - Exploring Further

The three elements we have been talking about all work together to create this card. The Star is the interaction of a source or pattern, the stars, an intermediary, the figure, who connects through their libation (the content of the pitchers), the world with the heavens.

> The Star's
> "Three Elements" are:
>
> What are the star(s)?
> Who is in the card?
> What is being poured out?

1. Do you believe in destiny?
2. What do you think about astrology?
3. When you need healing where, or to whom, do you look?
4. How would you know if something was destined to be?
5. What cycles do you observe in your life?
6. How do you discover/observe the patterns in your life?

When answering each of the questions for today, try to frame them in relationship to the three elements of The Star from Day 1.

Day 5 - Embodiment

Do the following. Do not worry. No one can see you, so just go for it!

Set a timer for eight minutes. Start chanting,

"Turn stars and speak. Pour your light into my life."

Just let it all fall into jumbles. If your tongue slips, then repeat the slip. If you make sounds, repeat them. Allow it to flow into blabbering.

When the timer sounds, make a note of whatever came up. See if anything needs to be added to your card from this exploration.

Without thinking, write down what gesture, or posture you see the figure taking on in this card.

If you need to gather more images, do so once you are done writing.

Day 6 - Looking at Elements

Review your images, words, and notes from this week's work. For each of the three elements, choose what you like most and least and explore how to include both in the card.

My rolls for this card were one star, a goddess, and wisdom. This fits well with my personal relationship to this card. We each have a star, guardian angel, or higher self that is set to guide us in life. It knows why we came to earth, who we are, and what we need to accomplish. In my studies of Kabbalah I would associate this with the Neshamah, in the ceremonial traditions I practice, the Holy Guardian Angel, or in the Lukumí tradition, Orí. So the idea of one star symbolizes this energy that connects with the infinite and resides outside of time and the world as being purely spiritual. The goddess on this card would be Sophia, the Gnostic goddess of wisdom, libating the world with her essence. The wisdom itself would be shown as light raining down from the vessel she carries. I would show only one pitcher to symbolize how wisdom unites.

Day 7 - Combining the Elements

Put it all together. Hopefully, you have a good idea of what is in and out of the card now. Remember that including the three elements in your card in some way will help solidify its meaning. The Star's three elements are: *What is/are the star(s)? Who is in the card? What is being poured out?* This is the day to create your card.

The Moon

Day 1 - Opening to Imagery

Draw a card and invoke your synchronicity. (Refer to the instructions in the "Synchronistic Whatchamacallit" section of the Introduction). Write down the card you drew.

Roll your die once for each of the lists below. (The number will tell you which of the options to include on your card.)

What is the Moon expressing?
1. Ennui
2. Grace
3. Angst
4. Fear
5. Hope
6. Fatigue

What animals/beings are in the centre of the card?
1. Two dogs
2. A cat and dog
3. An angel and devil
4. A man and woman
5. Two figures from other Trumps
6. Shadows of something off-screen

The Moon by Dy Langdon created using this process.

What is emerging from the water?
1. A crayfish
2. A fish
3. A snake
4. A crab
5. An alligator
6. A snail

As you work through this card, anytime you read "three elements" on another day's work, think back to these three questions and what the die chose for them.

Other elements you might consider including:

Are there two towers in the background? Guardians in the distance? Other lights in the sky? Other figures?

Find, sketch, or write out as many possibilities for each as you can. Make sure to leave enough time to do this for all three ideas.

Day 2 - Putting It in Perspective

Before reading today's work (below), please take a moment to write down any synchronous message(s) or cue(s) you have received as a result of the card you drew yesterday.

*****

The Moon is a card of shadows and the things we fear. This card is not the bright light of the goddesses, whom we find in the Priestess card, but it is a gate to the unconscious and the underground worlds of shadow. Here we face the unknown, the unknowable, our shadow, and our fears. This card speaks of being lost in the wild at night, without any clear way to be sure there is even still a path to walk.

The Moon itself in this card represents the emergence of light as a source of guidance. The Moon reflects back to us secrets and relationship to the divine. Will our connection to the divine carry us through our "dark night of the soul"? Is our spirituality waxing or waning? The face on the Moon reveals our hidden strength, or it can also highlight an existential crisis.

Many depictions of this card show two dogs in the centre. Sometimes they are fighting, other times they are hunting, and occasionally just menacing in the shadows. Often these animals represent our relationship to other people. Are they trying to lure us off the road for their own ends? Do they even register we are there, or are they just playing out their own dramas? Of course, these "dogs" might be old internalized voices, instead of people we know, now. It is obvious that to get where we are going the dogs must be dealt with in some manner.

The water in the foreground of this card stands for the unconscious, and from this dark pool usually emerges a crustacean of some sort. In places, this is described as a symbol of Christ bringing about the resurrection we find later in Judgement. We can read this symbol as a manifestation of our unconscious coming to influence us, for good or ill, depending on our relationship to it.

Day 3 - Working the Title

The Moon speaks of the possibility of renewal and rebirth after we pass through the challenges shown in this card.

1. What tools are best used on wild dogs?
2. Can the creations of a person's shadow be useful?
3. Is there a real danger in this card?
4. Who lives in the towers shown on this card?
5. Does it matter if the challenge in this card is real or imagined?

Look back over what you just wrote and note any words that stand out. Explore what other words you might use for this card. Grab a thesaurus if you want and explore other words that might cover the spectrum of ideas in this card more clearly for you. Of course, you can keep the traditional title if you like, too.

Day 4 - Exploring Further

The three elements we have been talking about all work together to create this card. The Moon is made of the emerging, though possibly obscured, light of spirit, the moon itself, forces emerging from within us, the Crayfish, and the worldly challenges, the dogs, usually brought about by the conflict between the celestial and the unconscious.

> The Moon's
> "Three Elements" are:
>
> What is the Moon expressing?
> What beings are in the middle?
> What is emerging from the water?

1. What guides you in life?
2. What could use renewal in your life?
3. What are you afraid of?
4. What parts of you might be trying to come to light that you are avoiding?
5. Who or what in your life acts like a pair of fighting dogs?
6. What or who blocks your path with their drama?
7. What force do you appeal to when you feel lost?

When answering each of the questions for today, try to frame them in relationship to the three elements of the Moon from Day 1.

Day 5 - Embodiment

Do the following. Do not worry. No one can see you, so just go for it!

Set a timer for eight minutes. Start chanting,

> **"Darkness that moves and breathes;**
> **darkness that yields so I can see."**

Just let it all fall into jumbles. If your tongue slips, then repeat the slip. If you make sounds, repeat them. Allow it to flow into blabbering.

When the timer sounds, make a note of whatever came up. See if anything needs to be added to your card from this exploration.

Without thinking, write down anything of note you see going on in this card.

If you need to gather more images, do so once you are done writing.

Day 6 - Looking at Elements

Review your images, words, and notes from this week's work. For each of the three elements, choose what you like most and least and explore how to include both in the card.

I rolled fatigue, two other Trump figures, and an alligator. I decided to choose the two players from other cards and went with Death and the Emperor. To me they represent the dance between control and the uncontrollable. Which leads to fatigue. Ultimately, this dance is an illusion since Death always wins. The alligator is Sebek, the Egyptian deity who devours the souls of the unworthy. He is the force of criticism and critical morality that seeks to stop my progress forward. Together they represent the need to move beyond control and fear of punishment to get past the fatigue that, at times, hits me on my journey.

Day 7 - Combining the Elements

Put it all together. Hopefully, you have a good idea of what is in and out of the card now. Remember that including the three elements in your card in some way will help solidify its meaning. The Moon's three elements are: *What is the Moon expressing? What beings are in the middle? What is emerging from the water?* This is the day to create your card.

The Sun

Day 1 – Opening to Imagery

Draw a card and invoke your synchronicity. (Refer to the instructions in the "Synchronistic Whatchamacallit" section of the Introduction). Write down the card you drew.

Roll your die once for each of the lists below. (The number will tell you which of the options to include on your card.)

What is the Sun?
1. A star
2. The visible face of God
3. An alien spaceship
4. Your soul
5. A lantern
6. The centre of our universe

Who are the two people in the card?
1. Children
2. Lovers
3. A child and a horse
4. The sun and moon
5. Adam and Eve
6. Your spirit and body

What is in the background?
1. A wall
2. A field
3. The expanse of space
4. A city
5. A farm
6. A forest

As you work through this card, anytime you read "three elements" on another day's work, think back to these three questions and what the die chose for them.

Other elements you might consider including:

What emotions are the people and Sun showing? Is something emanating from the Sun? Is there anyone else in the scene?

Find, sketch, or write out as many ideas for each as you can. Make sure to leave enough time to do this for all three ideas.

Day 2 - Putting It in Perspective

Before reading today's work (below), please take a moment to write down any synchronous message(s) or cue(s) you have received as a result of the card you drew yesterday.

*****

The Sun can speak of connection, playfulness, ease, and grace. It certainly tends to bode well for any question we put to it. It can show love, prosperity, health, and progress. It is a card that speaks of abundant times and the possibility of great harvests to come.

Without the sun there would be no life on earth. Its energy feeds the plants that support all the rest of the life on earth. Its warmth prevents the earth from being just a frozen rock whipping through the cosmos. How the sun shows up in this card, based on what you have rolled, reveals our relationship to the source of life. Spiritually speaking, is it within us or exterior to us? Does it wish us well, or is it ambivalent?

This card represents a level of connection and ease found in children and sages. The way the two figures relate to each other will explain a lot about what is going on in the card. Especially if we take them as two sides of the same person. Is there a division, or conflict between them? Are they innocent, or furtive? Is there love between them, or something else?

What is going on in this card happens outside of the daily world. In many decks, there is a wall behind the two figures, implying some kind of separation from the world. The nature of the division helps us understand their relationship to the world and the culture in which they find themselves. Is the world accepting, or judgemental towards them. A barbwire-topped fence tells a very different story than a rustic stone wall in a farmer's field.

Day 3 - Working the Title

The Sun speaks of nourishment, freedom, innocence, and exploration. It also speaks of our relationship to the divine.

1. How does one move past culture into a more direct connection with spirit?
2. What tools can help create good boundaries?
3. What value is there in innocence?
4. What role does spirit have in growing our lives?
5. What nourishes everyone?
6. If it feels good, is it okay?

Look back over what you just wrote and note any words that stand out. Explore what other words you might use for this card. Grab a thesaurus if you want and explore other words that might cover the spectrum of ideas in this card more clearly for you. Of course, you can keep the traditional title if you like, too.

Day 4 - Exploring Further

The three elements we have been talking about all work together to create this card. The Sun incorporates the interaction of a "higher" source, the sun itself and what it stands for, an earthly influence, the wall and what is beyond it, on a person or situation, the two figures.

> The Sun's
> "Three Elements" are:
>
> What is the Sun?
> Who are the two people?
> What is in the background?

1. How easy is your relationship to spirit?
2. How do the various parts of you relate to each other?
3. How at ease are you in relationship to the world you live in?
4. How playful are you?
5. How wise?
6. Where do you get your nourishment?

When answering each of the questions for today, try to frame them in relationship to the three elements of the Sun from Day 1.

Day 5 - Embodiment

Do the following. Do not worry. No one can see you, so just go for it!

Set a timer for eight minutes. Start chanting,

"Radiant life, blessed light, perfect summer's day."

Just let it all fall into jumbles. If your tongue slips, then repeat the slip. If you make sounds, repeat them. Allow it to flow into blabbering.

When the timer sounds, make a note of whatever came up. See if anything needs to be added to your card from this exploration.

Without thinking, write down what gesture or posture you see the figures taking on in this card. How are they interacting?

If you need to gather more images, do so once you are done writing.

Day 6 - Looking at Elements

Review your images, words, and notes from this week's work. For each of the three elements, choose what you like most and least and explore how to include both in the card.

I rolled the visible face of God, lovers, and a field. Certainly the first place my mind goes with this combination is to ponder the mysteries of what makes the crops grow. It is a very pagan combination that might be shown around the cycles of planting through to the harvest. For me, this card speaks of things that we only understand symbolically. Science can explain some of how this whole system works, but it lacks poetry. This card and this combination is poetic. God whispers, through the Sun, "Love each other and create the future." My card would show a couple embracing while the sun whispers poetry to them. Around them, plants grow and animals frolic. Crops sprout and bloom. A lush and abundant scene of play, connection, nourishing the future, and the mysteries of love.

Day 7 - Combining the Elements

Put it all together. Hopefully, you have a good idea of what is in and out of the card now. Remember that including the three elements in your card in some way will help solidify its meaning. The Sun's three elements are: *What is the Sun? Who are the two people? What is in the background?* This is the day to create your card.

Judgement

Day 1 - Opening to Imagery

Draw a card and invoke your synchronicity. (Refer to the instructions in the "Synchronistic Whatchamacallit" section of the Introduction). Write down the card you drew.

Roll your die once for each of the lists below. (The number will tell you which of the options to include on your card.)

Who is at the top of the card?
1. An angel
2. An ancestor
3. An alien
4. Your higher self
5. Anubis
6. The void

Who are the people at the bottom of the card?
1. Random folks
2. Parts of you
3. Friends and family
4. The chosen ones
5. Sinners
6. Just you

What is the figure at the top doing in relationship to the people?
1. Blowing a trumpet
2. Calling them to dinner
3. Yelling at them
4. Preaching to them
5. Healing them
6. Abducting them

As you work through this card, anytime you read "three elements" on another day's work, think back to these three questions and what the die chose for them.

Other elements you might consider including:

Are the figures all the same? Is there a grave? Where are they? How is the being at the top perched there?

Find, sketch, or write out as many ideas for each as you can.
Make sure to leave enough time to do this for all three ideas.

Day 2 - Putting It in Perspective

Before reading today's work (below), please take a moment to write down any synchronous message(s) or cue(s) you have received as a result of the card you drew yesterday.

*****

The Judgement card can represent an ending, or perhaps a call to a new level of being. It can often be thought of as the "end of days," the depiction of spirits being called to judgement for their actions. However, it can also be seen as a realigning with our nature. Crowley's Aeon card really shows this idea of bringing the whole of ourselves into a proper relationship with our purpose. Whether you see everything on this card as part of your inner life or as an external process will determine a lot about your card.

The being at the top of the card represents a higher level, reality, or consciousness. The way the angel is often shown is reaching out from the clouds indicates another place, beyond our sight, from which they are coming. The nature of the being shown here will reveal a whole spiritual cosmology. If it is Gabriel coming to blow the horn to raise the dead at the end of day, it has a very specific meaning. If it is your higher self calling, you to wake you up to a fuller level of awareness. The ideas are very different.

Often this card shows three figures at the bottom – a man, a woman, and a child. Who are they? Unconscious, conscious, and superconscious, possibly? Do they represent the legacy of your family and upbringing in your life? Perhaps they are just aspects of your personality. Their relationship to each other is important to defining the card. Is it just one of them being called out for judgement while the others watch? Do they care for each other?

The way in which the being at the top is acting towards the people at the bottom is the final piece of the equation. There is the manner of the interaction, but also the tone of it. The angel is blowing a horn, but is also revealing the glory of the spiritual world. Or perhaps it is not the glory, but fire and brimstone raining down, and the trumpet announces a punishment. When thinking about the action of this being, consider how the people at the bottom feel about it? What (if any) emotion is this being experiencing in relationship to what it is doing?

Day 3 - Working the Title

Judgement speaks of nourishment, freedom, innocence, and exploration. It also speaks of our relationship to the divine.

1. What is the point of life?
2. Does innocence of the rules matter?
3. How does karma work?
4. Are amends possible?
5. What can we do if others mistreat us?
6. What values do you judge the world by?

Look back over what you just wrote and note any words that stand out. Explore what other words you might use for this card. Grab a thesaurus if you want and explore other words that might cover the spectrum of ideas in this card more clearly for you. Of course, you can keep the traditional title if you like, too.

Day 4 - Exploring Further

The three elements we have been talking about all work together to create this card. Judgement is (a) a higher being, (b) the angel, communicating a divine message, the trumpet, to (c) creation, the people.

> Judgement's "Three Elements" are:
>
> Who is at the top of the card?
> Who is at the bottom of the card?
> What is the being at the top doing?

1. What judgements do others have of you that might have merit?
2. Do you believe in a higher power?
3. What happens after we die?
4. Are there parts of you that are out of alignment?
5. If you got a report card of your life right now, what would it say?
6. What is the code you wish to be measured by?

When answering each of the questions for today, try to frame them in relationship to the three elements of Judgement from Day 1.

Day 5 - Embodiment

Do the following. Do not worry. No one can see you, so just go for it!

Set a timer for eight minutes. Start chanting,

"End of days, end of time, eternal life of my soul."

Just let it all fall into jumbles. If your tongue slips, then repeat the slip. If you make sounds, repeat them. Allow it to flow into blabbering.

When the timer sounds, make a note of whatever came up. See if anything needs to be added to your card from this exploration.

Without thinking, write down what gesture or posture you see each figure taking on in this card. How are they interacting?

If you need to gather more images, do so once you are done writing.

Day 6 - Looking at Elements

Review your images, words, and notes from this week's work. For each of the three elements, choose what you like most and least and explore how to include both in the card.

My die rolls were the void, random folks, and abducting them. To me, the big questions in relationship to this card are: can we know the higher being? What does it take to wake people up? And is life random or pre-determined? In these rolls, I see suggestions of a very cynical answer. The source is beyond knowing; it is a void. People come together in a random way and interact with each other. It is a roll of the dice whether they are good for us or not. To top it off, these random humans are being abducted. It suggests there is some plan, but we are not privy to it. We must be taken forcibly to another place for reasons unknown. Maybe the *X-Files* had it right, and the world is a shadowy place full of mystery.

Day 7 - Combining the Elements

Put it all together. Hopefully, you have a good idea of what is in and out of the card now. Remember that including the three elements in your card in some way will help solidify its meaning. Judgement's three elements are: *Who is at the top of the card? Who is at the bottom of the card? What is the top being doing?* This is the day to create your card.

The World

Day 1 - Opening to Imagery

Draw a card and invoke your synchronicity. (Refer to the instructions in the "Synchronistic Whatchamacallit" section of the Introduction). Write down the card you drew.

Roll your die once for each of the lists below. (The number will tell you which of the options to include on your card.)

Who is in the centre of the card?
1. A woman
2. An angel
3. The galactic core
4. A baby
5. An alien
6. Nothingness

What are the four beings in the four directions?
1. Crystals
2. The four elements
3. A lion, an eagle, an angel, and an ox
4. The four archangels
5. Ancestors
6. Saints

What is between them?
1. A wreath
2. The gates to Eden
3. A rainbow
4. Outer space
5. Standing stones
6. The aura of the person in question

As you work through this card, anytime you read "three elements" on another day's work, think back to these three questions and what the die chose for them.

Other elements you might consider including:

What is the backdrop for this card? Are there figures beyond the ones rolled for here? Is something guiding this scene?

Find, sketch, or write out as many possibilities for each as you can. Make sure to leave enough time to do this for all three ideas.

Day 2 - Putting It in Perspective

Before reading today's work (below), please take a moment to write down any synchronous message(s) or cue(s) you have received as a result of the card you drew yesterday.

*****

The World card represents many things. As the final card in the series, it can show the end of a cycle or the attainment of a goal. It can show the proper order of things – a balance amongst head, heart, body, and soul, for example. It can represent the spiritual centre or core of things behind the manifest world. Balance, harmony, achievement, revelations, and structure are all found here.

In the centre of the card, we often find the person asking the question. What does it say about humanity that this figure is most often a naked woman dancing? The character that you find in your card will speak directly to your nature. Are you free of conditioning and karma, that is, "naked," in front of spirit? Is there a higher power implied by the being you rolled? What part of you is being called forth by this image? How is it desirable?

The four beings in the corners of this card are often related to a wide range of symbols. The angel, eagle, ox, and lion might represent Aquarius, Scorpio, Taurus, and Leo – or air, water, earth, and fire – or any of a wide range of other symbols. Collectively, they are complete. Together, they can balance each other and promote both growth and stability. If one dominates, it might undermine the whole system. What you place in these quarters speaks to a complete model of the self.

What is the divide between the being in the middle and those in the corners of the card? The wreath shown in older decks is a gentle boundary that seems constructed, or cultivated, like a hedgerow around a property. This element reveals a lot about the relationship between the central figure and the world around them. How easily could one of the beings in the corners approach the figure in the centre? Is their relationship supportive, protective, or antagonistic?

Day 3 - Working the Title

The World reveals the composition of our being and our relationship to the world.

1. What lessons does this card teach the world?
2. Is balance important?
3. Where is this card happening?
4. How does chaos or entropy fit into this card?
5. Is there a divine force guiding us to this place?

Look back over what you just wrote and note any words that stand out. Explore what other words you might use for this card. Grab a thesaurus if you want and explore other words that might cover the spectrum of ideas in this card more clearly for you. Of course, you can keep the traditional title if you like, too.

Day 4 - Exploring Further

The three elements we have been talking about all work together to create this card. The World is the four parts of the self, or creation, drawn into balance and harmony by the central figure, through the energy that is between them.

> The World's "Three Elements" are:
>
> Who is in the centre?
> What four beings are in the corners?
> What is between them?

1. If the four beings in the corners are people in your life, who are they?
2. What parts of you do you like best?
3. What parts do you dislike?
4. What brings harmony and flow?
5. If this card shows the goal of your life, what does that mean in a day-to-day way?
6. What is the higher level indicated by the central figure to you?

When answering each of the questions for today, try to frame them in relationship to the three elements of the World from Day 1.

Day 5 - Embodiment

Do the following. Do not worry. No one can see you, so just go for it!

Set a timer for eight minutes. Start chanting,

"Move me, protect me, guide me in the dance of life."

Just let it all fall into jumbles. If your tongue slips, then repeat the slip. If you make sounds, repeat them. Allow it to flow into blabbering.

When the timer sounds, make a note of whatever came up. See if anything needs to be added to your card from this exploration.

Without thinking, write down what gesture or posture you see each figure taking on in this card. How are they interacting?

If you need to gather more images, do so once you are done writing.

Day 6 - Looking at Elements

Review your images, words, and notes from this week's work. For each of the three elements, choose what you like most and least and explore how to include both in the card.

I rolled the galactic core, ancestors, and a rainbow. In the context of these rolls, to me, they speak of the journey of our souls. We start in some other place. I would call it "Orun," the Lukumí word for heaven. From there, we act as ancestors guiding those we are related to. At some point, we come to earth and live a life, hopefully guided well by our ancestors on the other side. When we are done, we return to Orun. The rainbow in my tradition is Oshumare, who governs, in part, the process of reincarnation. This spirit helps us travel between the other side and earth. The balance in this card comes from the revolving aspect of creation as we shift back and forth between receiving the guidance of the ancestors when we are incarnated and our role as guide when we are between incarnations.

Day 7 - Combining the Elements

Put it all together. Hopefully, you have a good idea of what is in and out of the card now. Remember that including the three elements in your card in some way will help solidify its meaning. The World's three elements are: *Who is in the centre? What are the 4 beings in the corners? What is between them?* This is the day to create your card.

*****

Oh, and by the way, congratulations! This is the last card! Finishing today's work means you have made it all the way to the end of the creation process, and soon you will be holding *your* very own deck in your hands. Way to go you – you are amazing!

Appendix

File Set-up

If you are going to use a printer or copy shop to make a physical copy of your deck, there are is a bit of terminology that would be helpful for you to know. Printing is easy these days. If the first place you go or call makes it seem complicated, find another business to work with. It is really simple.

Printer lingo

Here are some important terms you'll want to know when setting up your files, whichever printing method you use.

Trim: The actual final size of your cards when printed and cut to size.

Bleed: To account for shifting in the paper during trimming, images that go off the card require an extra 1/8th inch (or more).

Because I am unable to speak to all image editing software options, I will use Acorn

---

Printer terminology guidelines

When printing the paper can move some. Bleed, trim, and safety are used to make sure the art still looks good.

⟵ Trim size. *Everything outside this will get cut off.*

⟵ Bleed. *The extra printing that is trimmed but needed for images that go past the edge. Usually 1/8 inch outside the trim*

⟵ Safe area. *The line inside the trim area that can be guaranteed not to get trimmed due to shifts in the printing process. Usually 1/8 inch inside the trim*

Your printer will tell you what their guidelines are.

as my example. Other software will do the exact same thing, but the wording might be a bit different.

To see the file size click <image> on the top menu and choose <resize image>

If you look at the "image size" or "resize image," option it will tell you the dimensions (2.75" x 4.75") and a resolution size, too. Web images usually have a resolution of 72 pixels per inch. Print images are 300 per inch. When grabbing images online, always grab the biggest one you can (highest number of pixels) so it will print well. You can always scale them down, but scaling them up will make them grainy. **When working digitally, make sure your file is set to the correct size and the resolution is 300.**

If you are using art found online, be sure to note the source so you can give credit later on. You might think you'll be able to find it later, but it isn't always that simple.

Credits

My approach to card reading, which this book rests on, comes out of a few places. It has been shaped and refined in relationship to all the people I have read for over the years. All the conversations I've had with other readers – especially those on my podcast – have helped me to understand my own views more clearly.

I've read many books, but the most influential are the *Book of Thoth* by Aleister Crowley; *The Gaian Tarot* companion book by Joanna Powell Colbert; and *Tarot – The Open Reading* by Yoav Ben-Dov.

www.ingramcontent.com/pod-product-compliance
Lightning Source LLC
Chambersburg PA
CBHW070647160426
43194CB00009B/1612